Walking

MACMILLAN CARIBBEAN WRITERS

Walking

Joanne Haynes

MACMILLAN
CARIBBEAN

Macmillan Education
Between Towns Road, Oxford, OX4 3PP
A division of Macmillan Publishers Limited
Companies and representatives throughout the world

www.macmillan-caribbean.com

ISBN: 978-1-4050678-12

Typeset by EXPO Holdings
Cover design by John Barker
Cover images by Carole Ann Ferris

Thanks to the models for the front cover:
Sue Yen Douglas, the adult, Kezia Anderson, the child,
and the Cascade School for the Deaf, Trinidad,
for their helpful cooperation.   .

Printed and bound in Hong Kong

2011 2010 2009 2008 2007
10 9 8 7 6 5 4 3 2 1

Series Preface
Macmillan Caribbean Writers Series

Walking is a rites of passage novel about the sexual, personal, intellectual and creative development of an insecure but gifted young woman, from preschool freshness through adolescent sex and motherhood to artistic recognition. Set in Trinidad, this sensitive first novel reads as naturally and uninhibitedly as if the author is confiding in a close friend. New writer Joanne Haynes brings to vivid life the exaggerated horrors and humiliations experienced by a lonely, suppressed little girl; the turbulent spirit, self-centredness and obsessive angst of the teenage rebel; the continued introspection, confusion, doubts and questing of the unfulfilled adult.

The Macmillan Caribbean Writers Series (MCW) is an exciting collection of fine writing which treats the broad range of the Caribbean experience. The series offers a varied selection of novels and short stories, and also embraces works of non-fiction, poetry anthologies and collections of plays particularly suitable for arts and drama festivals.

As well as reviving well-loved West Indian classics and presenting new writing by established authors, MCW is proud to introduce work by newly discovered writers, such as Joanne Haynes, Martina Altmann, Deryck Bernard, Garfield Ellis, Joanne C. Hillhouse, Margaret Knight and Graeme Knott. Writers on the list come from around the region, including Guyana, Trinidad, Tobago, Barbados, St Vincent, Bequia, Grenada, St Lucia, Dominica, Montserrat, Antigua, the Bahamas, Jamaica and Belize.

MCW was launched in 2003 at the Caribbean's premier literary event, the Calabash Festival in Jamaica. Macmillan

Caribbean is also proud to be associated with the work of the Cropper Foundation in Trinidad, developing the talents of the region's most promising emerging writers, many of whom, such as Joanne Haynes, are contributors to MCW.

Judy Stone
Series Editor
Macmillan Caribbean Writers

Contents

Prologue

I used to wait every Saturday morning for the ice-cream boy to come up the road. When I heard the first, faint sounds of his bell in the street behind ours, I would run upstairs to my mother's room and pull out her pointy-toed, high-heeled black shoes, and slip them under my jersey, tiptoeing out of the room while looking out for Mummy or my tell-tale sister, Cleo. This done, I would hide the shoes under a chair in the living room, and go back outside to wait.

I would know from the sound of his bell exactly when he rounded the corner, and I would run inside, slide into my mother's shoes and wobble back out to the top of the driveway. Soon as I saw the bright red cap coming up the hill two houses before mine, I would put my hands on my hips and begin the jerky movements I called dance, attempting to keep time with the ping of his bell. My ankles and feet would rock in a different direction from the rest of my body, but the saucy grin I wore would give no testimony to the pain in my feet.

By the time Roger John came into view, I would be rocking and grinning, hoping each time he'd stop and talk to me. Somehow his bell always got louder and faster just before he reached my house, and I would find myself doing a sort of zigzag movement, compensating for the increased tempo by jerking my shoulders hard, since I could not move my high-heeled feet. Roger John's cart at the front of his bike would sway sharply from side to side, and I wished for it to fall so he would have to stop. He would scowl at it, as if warning it not to, and, just after he

1

passed my gate, he would turn the same look upon me, push his cap back, and shout, "Yuh fresh lil girl!"

I would grin and continue my frenzied movement until I could see the red cap reach the top of the hill that took him out of Lazzari Street, then I would limp back inside, take the shoes off, and sneak them back to their rightful place, now remembering to be frightened lest I was caught.

I must have really been a 'fresh' little girl, because my sisters swear I was no more than five at the time. But there's always been this spirit in me – a spirit that has both put me in trouble and saved my life; a spirit that many have tried to tame, that I myself have disguised and hidden so often that I sometimes forget what it looks like, and am wonderfully surprised when I dig into my folds of fear and conformity to find it there, waiting, like a burst of orange colour in a sea of safe, drab grey.

Part One

On Angels' Wings

"Heaven must have been quite empty when I was growing up"

Josephine Chin

Mrs Simmons

This spirit was bleached, starched and ironed into a neat, ribboned package and delivered to St Maria's Girls' Catholic School. My crazy, curly hair was Vaselined into two plaits, each safely anchored by a perfectly tied green bow, my inner white blouse was starched so much the sleeves stuck out from my skinny arms like right-angle triangles, and my shoes and socks were so white they hurt my eyes.

But my insides were crumpled.

My stomach was swollen from lumpy porridge and constipation, my heart was balled up and afraid to beat, and my palms were so sweaty they left wet spots wherever I touched. I followed my mother into the school, feeling as grey inside as the walls.

Corridor after corridor we walked, until my mother stopped, pushed me forward, patted my head, turned and crossed into the courtyard to get to her classroom.

Slowly I looked up from the fat, stockinged feet before me, up into eyes that reached from behind their glasses into my heart, eyes that smiled wider than her mouth. She reached out and took my hand, held it between hers and wiped off the sweat with her smooth, dry fingers.

"Good morning, Josephine. I'm Mrs Simmons."

As she stroked my hand, my insides began to smoothen out like the rest of me, as if her actions ironed me, on the inside. I met her eyes, and smiled.

And knew then that angels do exist.

And so it was every morning. I would reach to school earlier than the other girls because my mother taught there; and by the time the others had arrived I'd erased the blackboard, sharpened pencils and drawn so many pictures on the blackboard that my insides were as pristine as my outsides.

Until I saw the threatening figure of Sister Angelica walking down the corridor, or heard her voice come over the public address system. Then my stomach would dive into my bladder and fill me with the uncontrollable need to pee.

Sister Angelica threatened us with the wrath of God, which seemed to live in her leather strap. We were bullied into maintaining pure lily-white souls and, blinded by her white gown and dead white skin, we could not help but think that white was what we should be. She would appear like a ghost on the corridor, causing a sudden collective quiet as we waited to see which devil would be exorcized by her leather strap. Her flat, cold eyes made me tremble in every corner of my body, but when they glinted with sudden life as she lifted our skirts to belt us, I feared her even more.

We could be punished for anything: from doing badly in a test, to eating foods that were not healthy, to playing too roughly and injuring ourselves. And all the while she whipped, she ranted about the Devil and letting him get into our souls. We were warned of the Devil trying to trick us into playing wildly, the Devil hiding in our laziness, our carelessness, our untidiness.

I found myself looking more for the Devil than I did for God. For I knew now that the Devil could be anywhere: in the mischievous pranks of a five-year-old, in a dirty shoe, even in a book forgotten at home, and he was the more dangerous because I could not see him. It seemed to me the Devil hid himself from me and only appeared when Sister Angelica came around, just to get me into trouble. Like the time she belted me for forgetting my math book at home. I could see the Devil grinning and

6

winking at me from the cover of my book left on the dining table, yet somehow Sister Angelica, with every stroke she delivered, seemed to be seeing him right there, on my bottom; for when she was done, I could see him no more. In fact, I could see nothing through the blur of my teary eyes.

And even though we were told that God was everywhere, it seemed to me that He got upstaged by the Devil, for we saw far less of Him.

This confusion filled my thoughts. If God was so powerful, how come the Devil was always there? Tapping at our backs and making us do the things that got us in trouble? I began to realize that after the Devil's temptation came, licks always followed. I surmised that the Devil probably had to be beaten out, and I learnt well Sister Angelica's famous quote: "After joy comes sorrow."

Putting all these clues together, I summed up that the Devil must live in our spirit, for always a beating came after any show of spirit, whether it came in the form of a rowdy game of catch or in the blurting out of a truthful answer such as "I forgot", when asked the seemingly innocent question of "Why were you seen running and laughing like a fish-wife during breaktime?"

It seemed the children who bowed their heads and looked contrite were punished less severely, sometimes not at all, even though we all knew they were faking.

So I tried hard to keep the Devil out by holding my spirit in; if he didn't see it, how could he get in? So I would play in spurts, laugh in spurts, and then, remembering, look around, suddenly panicked that he might have already come without my realizing or, worse yet, that Sister Angelica, always on the lookout for him, would now be bearing down on me, having seen him slip by without my knowing.

And I would stop my joy, so that sorrow could not come.

Had it not been for Mrs Simmons, I might have been turned into an atheist. In fact, I was so afraid of God's wrath and so doubtful of His power to stop the Devil from invading me that I found myself gravitating toward Jesus. The stories told to us about Jesus by Mrs Simmons left me with the quiet assurance that Jesus's love was not conditional like His Father's, and at nights I found myself omitting God and praying to his Son.

But even Mrs Simmons could not stop the teasing I got for the problem I developed. Somehow the Devil had found his way into my bladder, and I would find myself pressing and shifting on my seat, as much surprised as Mrs Simmons by my sudden urge to pee. When I did get up to go, I would be squeezing my legs together and trying to run at the same time, which resulted in a sort of gallop that would send the class into waves of laughter, bringing the pee down my legs before I got to the toilet. Since we weren't allowed to run down the corridor I would try to control myself enough to walk, leaving a trail of urine behind me. As soon as I was out of sight of the teachers whose classrooms faced the courtyard I would bolt, so that the trail became separate drops. My only comfort would be the sound of Mrs Simmons's voice as she scolded the class for laughing at me. But this comfort was fleeting, for the shame would continue as I was seen, from all the other classes on the bottom floor, mopping the corridor.

Somehow Mrs Simmons learnt to read a look of panic that I didn't even know was on my face, and she would send me to the toilet quickly. Then she started sending me on errands, telling me to use the bathroom before I returned. From the time the PA system came on, Mrs Simmons would look at me and point her finger toward the corridor, and I would find that, by the time Sister Angelica's voice came on, I would be squeezing my legs together and walking as briskly as I could, suddenly desperate for the toilet. So that was how I controlled it, but Mrs Simmons could do nothing when Sister Angelica suddenly appeared by our classroom door and thirty-nine heads turned in my direction, snickering quietly, straining to watch the pee seep onto the floor.

So that was how my first year of school began: my faith barely restored by Mrs Simmons, my five-year-old mind in constant worry about the Devil, doubting the existence and power of God. And in the evenings, at home, I would feel the need to beat my dolls while repeating the lessons on sin I had heard during the day until, suddenly tired and fed up, I would drop the ruler and go outside and sit on the swing, whose rocking, after some time, made me remember the other lessons, the quiet, loving ones of Mrs Simmons, and eventually, I would be swinging high and singing, joined once again by my spirit.

Until my mother's voice called me inside.

Michelle Brown

Michelle Brown could hardly be considered an angel. In fact she was more like an imp; but the laughter she brought to my world, and the fact that she took so much pressure off me, made me grateful to her.

Michelle Brown came to our school in Second Year Infants. This set her immediately apart, since friendships had already been forged and St Maria's girls were not known for being friendly to outsiders. We soon discovered another thing about Michelle Brown that made her more strange – she was bursting with spirit!

I feared for her life.

Every time her hand rose to ask the questions I was afraid to, I trembled. As if this wasn't bad enough, Michelle Brown was black, and not even Catholic! I secretly admired her, her boldness, her mischief, but Lord! I worried for her. For now there was no Mrs Simmons to shelter Michelle Brown; we were faced instead by the dour Mrs Waters. I knew Michelle Brown was destined for trouble, and though I liked her, I waited with the feeling of the inevitable dread to come.

One time Mrs Waters asked if we knew who Dr Eric Williams – the Father of Our Nation – was. Michelle Brown's hand shot up, and before Miss could call her, she was standing and asking, in her loud, clear voice, "Doeth that mean he ith all of uth father? He'th not my father. My father ith ..."

Mrs Waters was upon her, ruler in hand; she swung Michelle Brown around and delivered three hard strokes to the back of her legs. As the second lash hit her, Michelle Brown made the connection between her words and her pain and her mouth snapped shut like a flytrap. Her eyes filled with tears, but not a drop fell. The incident kept her quiet for the rest of the morning, but by lunchtime she was asking to join games and she raised her hand four times that evening, though Mrs Waters ignored her each time.

And so it went; of the ten or twelve times that hand went up each day, it was noticed once, sometimes not at all.

And now Mrs Waters encouraged us to tease Michelle Brown, as she'd roll her eyes and say, in a tired voice, "Yeth, Michelle Brown?" mocking the tie-tongue she knew the other girls teased Michelle Brown about. She'd look around at the class, grinning, and receiving the expected laughter and giggles. Still, this did not stop Michelle Brown. Eagerly she'd jump to her feet, her straightened plaits bouncing against her back and forgetting to bounce back down, even while their enormous ribbons flapped down, and in her strong, confident voice, give her answer, grinning with the class even while they laughed at her.

At the back of the class I would grin too, but I was grinning with Michelle Brown, not against her. I was grinning for the boldness and bravery she showed, that I dared not. I was grinning for that spirit in her that sang and swung, no matter what. And mostly, selfishly, I was grinning because Michelle Brown often made Mrs Waters forget me.

Other than the times I wet myself and our teacher led the class in laughter, or the times when she would spitefully call out "Spelling test!" and look at me with gleeful hatred, knowing that the fear those two words put in me brought the Devil stamping down on my bladder and I'd be wetting myself halfway through the test, other than those times, Mrs Waters focused her energy on Michelle Brown, who seemed not at all afraid of the Devil. And still Michelle Brown would come to play at breaktimes and lunchtimes. Taller, stronger and tougher, she'd play so well that each time she asked, she would be told, "Yes".

So this love–hate relationship continued with the class and Michelle Brown. Encouraged by our teacher, some teased and taunted. We liked her from afar, for we knew that, for our safety, befriending Michelle Brown was bad news. But her quickness with answers, her boldness to ask questions, her jokes and pranks brought us relief, and no amount of jeering and threatening from Mrs Waters could stop the admiration we felt for this girl. The Devil seemed to have taken up permanent residence in Michelle Brown's spirit, and she didn't seem to mind.

Secretly, I thought the Devil must not be so bad, for Michelle Brown was tough and smart and brave.

Until the day under the cherry tree.

The only respite in any week of terror was the Friday afternoon, when we got to go under the cherry tree for reading. This happened so rarely that it was a wonderful treat. Mrs Waters used it as a powerful tool for undermining the hated and extolling the beloved.

"I was going to take you all under the cherry tree this week, but since Josephine did so horribly on her spelling test, the whole class will be punished."

And forty pairs of eyes full of hatred would be cast my way, while I bent my head, still able to see the smirk on my teacher's face.

At other times it would be, "Since Susan sang so beautifully this morning, you all get to go under the cherry tree today."

And smiles and sighs would be delivered to Susan, who would float off her seat like a proud, pretty butterfly.

On this fated day, the heat was the welcome deliverer of this gift. Happily, we picked up our reading books and formed a line, careful to be quiet and orderly, lest the privilege be revoked. Mrs Waters called Michelle Brown to bring her chair. She tottered in front of us while Mrs Waters took her time finding the perfect spot. Finally, after much looking up and assessing the shade,

Mrs Waters pointed to a spot right under the tree, and sat down. We waited to be told to sit, while Mrs Waters looked around, pointing and calling her pets forward while pretending to do a random search as, foolishly, we waved and tiptoed to get her attention. This done, we were instructed to sit, the usual children at the front.

As always, we sat in a half-circle, Mrs Waters in front and above, much, she used to say, like the Holy Spirit.

There was a beautiful, calming breeze, it was a few minutes before home time, and we were lulled into comfort. Mrs Waters began reading, we following the story in our books. As we were about to turn the first page, Michelle Brown, sitting next to me, called out in her loud, heavy voice, "Mith! Mith! A jep on yuh head!"

Our heads lifted.

Mrs Waters jumped up, dusting frantically at her chair. "Where? Where?" she cried, twisting swiftly from front to back, all the while dusting her chair.

"There, Mith! There, on yuh head!"

We craned our necks to see the jep, while Mrs Waters jumped from one foot to the other, giving sharp, quick taps to her head, shouting, "Where? Where?"

Michelle Brown jumped up, pointing. Those of us in the back jumped up too and, though none of us had seen it, Mrs Waters looked wildly from one to the other, shouting, "Where? Where?", hitting and shaking her head as she jumped from foot to foot.

And then her hair fell off.

It landed on Susan's lap. She jumped up, screaming.

We screamed too, laughing and pointing at Mrs Waters's battered wig on the ground, while our teacher, unaware of the joy in our screams, took them as an indication of our seeing the still hidden jep. She began shaking her head frantically – reminding me of my dog, Gypsy, after a bath – all the while she continued hitting it sharply, unaware that it was now made up of tiny little plaits pointing in all directions.

Thoroughly uncontrollable now, our screams turned into wails of laughter that suddenly registered on Mrs Waters, who looked at us, confused.

And then Michelle Brown shouted, "All Fool'th Day!"

Our teacher's hand froze just before impacting with her head again, as the screams of laughter fully hit her, and she looked down and saw her wig. She stared at Michelle Brown with so much hatred, that our laughter collectively ceased. Michelle Brown, head thrown back in glorious mischief, did not see the look on our teacher's face, did not see Mrs Waters charging towards her as we, silently, hurriedly, made room. Mrs Waters grabbed Michelle Brown by the collar and lifted her off the ground. Laughter still rocked Michelle Brown's body, even as her eyes opened wide in surprise. Mrs Waters spun her, slammed her to her feet, lifted her, spun her, and then, as she planted her down again, one heavy fist slammed into Michelle Brown's back. And another. And another.

They were moving in a kind of circle, she charging into Michelle Brown with blows and resounding slaps, as Michelle Brown tried to run around her, covering whatever spot had been hit, while Mrs Waters aimed and hit whatever spot she could find. For the first time, Michelle Brown cried. Loud, gasping breaths and wails that made every one of us want to cry too. Tears soaked her cheeks, neck, blouse, and she screamed, over and over, "Mith! I thorry! Mith!"

We stared in total fear as this morbid dance continued to the beat of Michelle Brown's pleas until, spent, Mrs Waters finally stopped. Panting, clothes askew, she looked down at Michelle Brown, crouched on the ground like a dog. Mrs Waters grunted, straightened her clothes, marched up to the wig on the ground. She planted it on her head, leaving one little plait still out, and stamped towards the classroom.

Silently, we followed, looking back at Michelle Brown, sobbing on the ground.

And that was the end of the cherry tree trysts. The end, too, of Michelle Brown.

An enormous black policeman came to our school the next day. Mrs Waters returned from the Principal's office looking satisfied, as Sister Angelica could be seen and heard escorting Michelle Brown and her father, whose uniform counted for nothing here, out of the school.

So I was left to face the torture of Mrs Waters alone. But I never forgot Michelle Brown, or what happened to her that day, and I knew, from then, that one's spirit could be a dangerous thing.

Maria and Antonia

By the time I got to Standard One, I'd become accustomed to living on the outskirts of life at St Maria's. Some days were better than others, as I would play with someone or be entertained by the older girls in my mother's class, but I can't really remember having friends.

Not until Maria and Antonia came to our school.

From the first day, Maria and Antonia set themselves apart. Maria, because she was white, and white girls did not go to our school, they went to private school, and Antonia, because she was an aristocrat who showed no interest in the snobs who tried to befriend her. Both were embarrassed by any favouritism shown by teachers or Principal, and so they were ostracized. Within the first week of their coming, I wet myself when Sister Angelica walked in on us. As I returned, shamefaced, with the mop, I noticed two faces that were not grinning and giggling like the others. We were drawn to each other, and by the end of the first term we were inseparable.

For the first time I had friends with whom I shared secrets. The story of Roger John, burning inside me like an ember, burst into flames one day when Maria confessed to having a crush on her neighbour. My Saturday morning pastime came to life and grew, as this version had Roger John smiling and winking back at me. We whispered, giggled and held hands, strolling through the courtyard at break and lunchtimes, sealing ourselves and each other against the teacher's tormenting and the sneers of the other girls.

One day, calling Antonia "Tony" took us to a new level of friendship.

Her eyes filled with tears, and she whispered, "Don't ever call me that again."

We found out that day that her dad, who had died when she was five, used to call her that. Then came my story that my father didn't live with us; that he lived with another woman; that I came from a broken home. This was a shocker, because everyone had been told, as instructed by my mother, that my father was dead. Next came Maria's story, that her highly qualified father was being supported by her mother because the judiciary kept 'losing' his papers, that he'd brought his family proudly home from England, to live in the most prestigious neighbourhood, and they were ignored and snubbed because they were the only blacks there.

Perhaps we knew too much about why we could not fit in with the others; too much pain, too much truth; too much to laugh at a seven-year-old's bowed head, as she watched her pee form a circle between her feet.

We buffered each other so well that I cannot remember many of the pains of Standard One. Our teacher tried everything to stop our friendship; while other friends were encouraged to sit together, we were constantly separated; if I did not know the answer to a question, the teacher would ask Antonia or Maria, and encourage the class to laugh at my stupidity, trying to urge smiles from my friends, who would look at her blankly. When everything failed, Antonia and Maria found themselves now on the wrong side of our teacher, amongst the ridiculed and scorned. Still this did not stop our friendship.

So now, when my stomach knotted in the mornings, I would remember my two friends and hold out till the precious bell rang for break and lunch. And every day I wondered why they had chosen me, when they could have been friends with anyone.

When they could have been teacher's pet. When they could have had life easy. Instead, they chose me. Surely, this could not be easier than just being a snob or being white? It never occurred to me that perhaps it was not a question of choice, that perhaps they just liked me.

I knew why Antonia and Maria were set apart, they chose to be, but I never understood what set me apart. I knew it had something to do with my mother being a teacher there, but there were other girls whose mothers taught there and, unlike me, they were popular. But there was always this name 'Chin' that came along with the sneers; the stares at my 'dada head', as my more Chinese-looking sisters referred to my hair; the questioning looks of the Attongs and Lees. I felt there were other things, too.

Now that we were in Standard One, we were considered old enough to sweep the corridors, a task, as stated by Sister Angelica, designed to keep us humble like Jesus. My first day sweeping, the girls started coming around, laughing and nudging each other. I tried to ignore them, then first one, then another, put her foot in front of my moving broom.

"Look how she sweeping!" Laughter.

"Like she 'fraid the broom!" Laughter.

"Like she 'fraid the ground!" Laughter.

Carrie Escott, our teacher's niece, ran into the classroom. "Auntie! Come! Come!"

Mrs Trottingham came to the door.

"Look!" said Carrie, pointing at me. "Look how Josephine sweeping!"

The girls around laughed and looked to our teacher for approval. She glared at me and then turned away.

"So?" she said to Carrie. "You can't sweep either!"

"Yes!" said Carrie. "Yes, I can!"

Mrs Trottingham grabbed the broom from Carrie's hand.

"No!" she shouted. "No! You can't! Come inside!"

Carrie looked around stupidly, then she bent her head and began tracing circles on the ground with the tip of her shoe. No one looked up. Only me. In amazement I looked at my teacher, shocked that she had picked up for me, I ventured a smile. She cut her eyes at me and walked off, dragging Carrie behind her.

I thought this meant a new chapter in life between me and my teacher, but somehow, it made things worse. I was now treated with a type of scorn I could not understand, as if Mrs Trottingham somehow hated and envied me at the same time. I could not understand this. But my confusion was washed away at each break and lunchtime, and I learned to be as happy as I could in these short times, for I knew the truth of "after joy comes sorrow".

This new treatment by Mrs Trottingham made my bladder more uneasy than ever. Sometimes she would just have to look my way and I would begin gyrating on my seat. And this is what Mrs Trottingham did: knowing my terror of spelling tests, knowing that I ran to the toilet every evening after prayers, she started giving spelling tests last thing before the final bell. The combination was too much. Word after word, I would write stupidness, as all my concentration went to squeezing my legs and trying to stop the hateful pee that was coming anyway. Evening after evening, the whole lower school would see me walking across to Infants to get the mop, the back of my skirt wet. My only consolation was the kind, sympathetic looks of Maria and Antonia. One day, even before Mrs Trottingham said those two dreaded words, my bladder filled suddenly, in anticipation, and desperation made me bold. Raising my hand, halfway off my seat, I cried,

"Miss! Miss! May I please go to the bathroom?"

Mrs Trottingham looked at me, seemed to consider my request. I waited hoping, holding my breath, praying. The teacher looked at the giant clock on the wall.

"Wait for the bell." Then: "Spelling test."

And I could not, this time, make it only trickle. The pee gushed from me as I sat with only one half of my bottom on the seat, wrote nothing, and saw a sea of shaking shoulders before me, the sound of my pee hitting the floor pounded in my ears. And then I stood, as one of five, in front the class, hand extended, waiting for my three strokes for each wrong word. I had written none of the ten words. Mrs Trottingham held her nose as she came to stand in front me, looked back at the class, who roared with laughter, all except two.

"Phew!" she said, holding her nose tight. "This classroom smelling bad."

She looked back at the class again. "Maybe somebody have to help you clean up this mess this time."

And there they were, Maria and Antonia, jumping up, both saying, "I will!"

"Sit down!" snapped Mrs Trottingham, turning to deliver my punishment. I felt none of the lashes, instead I felt the pain in my friends' eyes.

The laughter was so loud as I made my trek to Infants that day that even teachers' heads popped out of their doors. I was so ashamed, I made my way to Mrs Simmons's class by memory, for I dared not look up to see where I was going. As I tried to grab the mop and leave without Mrs Simmons seeing the back of my skirt, walking sideways then backwards, I saw her feet in front me.

"Josephine, you still wetting yourself?" she asked of my bent head. Her hand lifted my chin and, as she always used to, she pulled me in with her eyes. "You're a big girl now. You hear?"

I nodded.

"It's time to stop this."

Nod.

Her voice changed, no longer kind and soft. Her eyes changed, they pressed into mine, into me, somewhere deep inside. "You hear me, Josephine? You have to stop this."

I nodded, in a hurry to escape, hurt and confused by her tone. She stepped back, smiled. I grabbed the mop and fled.

And then, a few days later, something happened that made me love Mrs Simmons all over again. Sister Angelica's haunting figure floated into our classroom. Her cold eyes surveyed us as we scrambled to stand and say, eloquently, even while we trembled inside, "Good morning, Sister."

She nodded, turned to Mrs Trottingham, asked about the progress and behaviour of the class. Mrs Trottingham looked around, called a few of her favourites, told Sister about their excellent development, all the while sneaking wicked peeps at me. My classmates nudged each other and waited.

Waited for the eruption of Josephine.

My stomach had long ago lurched, my bladder screamed, and as I fidgeted around on my seat, I heard a voice far away, yet inside me, saying, *You have to stop this.*

And Mrs Simmons's eyes, their look of love and disappointment and hope, suddenly made sense, and I found myself sitting still, tensely at first, then easily, as I realized my stomach had gone back to its usual place, and my bladder had stopped screaming.

Suddenly, I knew I was not going to wet myself. And I sat back in my seat; felt the questions, outrage, and pride of two. As Sister Angelica walked out, the amazement of teacher and class was like a massive breath, holding us all in a moment of dead silence. Mrs Trottingham looked at me with pure hate.

Then she spat, "Spelling test!"

My stomach lurched, my face revealed a look that brought sheer glee to my teacher's eyes. And then, something else kicked inside me. Some power that had been released, some power found.

And everything settled.

And I felt Mrs Simmons smile.

It was lucky for me that this power came when it did for, shortly afterwards, first Maria, then Antonia, told of their families' intentions to move. I was devastated! We tried to console each other, telling each other we'd remain friends, but we knew already that life could not always be trusted, and that people, with the best intentions, could not always keep their promises.

So we smiled and talked and played, but all the while we waited and watched the term, and with it our friendship, come to an end. For the first time in my entire life, I dreaded the end of term; and, of course, this time it came too fast. We cried and cried and said our goodbyes.

And I waited throughout the holidays, with great dread, to see what Standard Two, on my own again, would bring.

Double Power

Mrs White never showed her dislike of me openly, as my other teachers had. All the while she smiled at me, there was a smell of dislike, and this made me terribly uneasy. I had grown accustomed to blatant dislike, but this underlying feeling of distaste was beyond me. She would do things such as find my one book with the ratty cover (which was actually my scrap book), and hold it up, away from her, screwing her face up in distaste, and enquire innocently of the class:

"Now what kind of child would have a book looking like this?"

And every head in the class would turn towards me while she said, innocently, "Oh, Josephine? Is this yours?" Leaving me the choice of owning up or lying; and the hated book would be thrown at me.

Another time she lectured us about being grateful for the things we took for granted. Telling us a story about a girl with no hands, she made us each place a book on our desk and try to move it without using our hands. All the while she was smiling at our useless efforts, talking about humility and being like Jesus. Most of the class had given up by the time I eventually managed to slide my book and hold it up by pressing it between my neck and my chin.

Pet Susan, suitably impressed, shouted, "Look, Miss! Josephine did it!"

Mrs White gave me a sour look and said briskly, "Right! Time to stop playing the fool! Take out your math books."

My victory slid from under my chin and into my stupid throat, which grew swollen with the threat of tears.

This was the kind of mean Mrs White was, a less obvious but far more deadly mean than I'd ever encountered, and I didn't know what to do. Having had Maria and Antonia made it worse, for I'd known the sweetness of their friendship, and missed them sorely now. And Mrs White's tactics made me uncomfortable. I was accustomed to being afraid, but I did not know how to handle this undercover brutality. The worst part was that I would be in her class for two years, up until Standard Four.

Then something happened that made me a hero for a few days.

My mother would sometimes take my sister, Cleo, and me home for lunch. On this day, we got home and she parked the car at the top of the steep driveway as usual. We got out and as we started walking down the hill, some instinct made me look back, and I saw the car rolling slowly down the hill towards us.

I jumped to the side, yelling, "Mom! Mom! Look! The car rolling!"

Mummy spun round as the car, picking up speed, headed for the pillar of our house. She ran to the door, grabbed the handle and opened it, but the car was moving too fast and she could not get in.

"Oh God!" she screamed. "It going to hit the house!"

We stood by, helpless. She reached through the window and grabbed the steering wheel, as the car dragged her along and her legs buckled with the speed. Half running, dragging alongside it, almost on her knees, she turned the wheel hard and fast, and we saw the car turning, slowly, off the driveway, into the grass, into the coconut tree. It slammed into the tree and finally stopped, throwing my mother to the ground, her wig flying into the air and landing on the car bonnet. Truly scared, we ran up to her as our maid, Rosie, came running outside.

"Miss Chin!"

"Mummy!"

My mother half sat, half lay on the ground, still holding the side of the car, her eyes opened wide in terror. My sister and I were crying.

"Mummy … Mummy," we said over and over.

And then my mother started to cry. Loud, horrible sobs that scared me more than her silence.

"Come, Miss Chin. Come," said Rosie, sliding her arm around my mother and trying to get her up. "Help her, girls."

Gingerly we touched our mother, afraid that her crumpled skirt and twisted legs meant worse injury even than the awful purple and black bruises we could already see forming along her shins. We lifted Mummy, who had stopped crying, though that shattered look stayed on her face. As we held her limping to the house, she stopped and looked back.

"Oh God!" she said. "Look at the car!"

We looked at the back of the car, crumpled like paper, jammed into the trunk of the tree.

"Oh God! Oh God! How I paying to fix that?" My mother started crying again, this time with long, angry tears.

Rosie turned her away, "Doh worry 'bout dat now, Miss Chin. Come. Yuh have to get inside and lie down."

My mother sobbed as she had the day I found out my doll's hair would not grow back. We practically toted her, her body heavy and limp. Yet when she got inside she refused to lie down, snapped that she didn't need a doctor, only sat looking terrified, asking over and over, "How I going to fix that?"

Someone called the doctor, who came and gave my mother some tablets that, mercifully, put her to sleep. Only then did the question for which we had no answer stop. My sister and I sat huddled on our mother's bed, guilty for every bad thought we'd ever had about her, and for that moment Cleo and I felt a bond with each other we never had before; for though we were at the same school, our five-year age difference and constant vying for our mother's attention had kept us from becoming close, so that I had never turned to her in any crisis, at home or at school, as one might have turned to an older sister.

The good side of this incident was that I was regarded with an awe by the other girls that I had never felt before. The word had got around that it was me who'd seen the car coming. Me who'd saved my mother's life. Apparently, even me who'd pulled my mother out of the way of the speeding car. In our few days' absence, Sister Angelica had announced over the PA system that we'd been in an accident. The entire school had prayed for us. She arranged a car to pick us up and drop us home while our car was being fixed – a simple act of calling the insurance company, efficiently organized by my older sister, Bernie, who, on coming home from the bank later that day of our accident, was able finally to answer and end my mother's ongoing question, "How I going to fix that?"

Yet when we did return to school and Sister Angelica came up to me to ask how I was, I shivered inside. And though she smiled, there was no warmth in that smile, as there was in the hug I got from Mrs Simmons. The girls crowded around me, asking for the story over and over, their eyes opening wide, some trying to cover grins when I talked about the wig. For a few days everyone called me, asked me to sit with them at lunch, came to see if I got the work I missed. Of course, it didn't last. For Mrs White's watchful eye always called them do something or to go somewhere when she saw them with me. After a few weeks, I was back to normal in popularity – none.

My mother became even more scared to drive after that. For days after the car was fixed and returned home, my mother continued using the services supplied by Sister Angelica, passing the car in the driveway, giving it looks of hate and hurt. When she finally got back into the driver's seat, her anxiety was so great, it filled the car with a dread so potent we felt as if a cloud hung over us.

School was awful, made more so now that I knew what was missing. Every day I wondered about Antonia and Maria, and I wondered if they wondered about me. I didn't know how I was going to survive, what with the excess tension in the mornings in the car, Mrs White's subtle, dangerous hatred, and my loneliness.

Then Mrs Edwards bustled into my life and lent me her wings.

Mrs Edwards was a short, plump, half-Chinese woman who involved herself thoroughly in school life, organizing tea parties and cake sales, all with the goal of raising funds for our school. This of course made her presence always welcome, and gave her rank and authority. She was allowed into our school at any time, and could take as many girls as she needed out of class to help her with the errands that kept our good Catholic school running efficiently. Mrs Edwards, we were told, was a true example of doing God's work.

Because her daughter was now in my class, Mrs Edwards would always pop her head into our class and ask for helpers from here.

Mrs White would make a good show of looking around, pretending to make a fair choice, while we raised our hands and called, "Miss! Me, Miss! Me!"

For going with Mrs Edwards was a treat! The girls who'd gone with her the previous year always came back showing off:

"Mrs Edwards took us for pizza."

"Mrs Edwards took us all over the place!"

"Mrs Edwards let us eat the extra cake that didn't sell!"

I longed to go with this exciting, full-of-fun woman, but time after time, as Mrs White always chose her pets to go, I realized it would never be. Sometimes Mrs White's eyes would focus on me so long, I felt sure I'd be picked, but always it was the same: Susan, Gillian, Lisa, Michelle, Donna, Theresa and of course, Elizabeth, Mrs Edward's daughter.

Mrs Edwards would smile and wave, saying, "Okay! Thanks, Miss! That's enough!"

And the rest of us would sag like wilted flowers, while our teacher looked around brightly and said, "Okay! Back to work!"

After this happened quite a few times, and I realized that the same five or six girls were always called, I began to put less effort into my waves and calls, knowing my status.

Then one day, after Mrs White had called out her clan, Mrs Edwards stayed by the door. She looked at me, then at Mrs White, and said, "And Josephine. Send Josephine."

Mrs White's smile faded, she gaped at Mrs Edwards as she stood by the door, waiting. My stomach danced and it took all my control not to jump up and hug Mrs Edwards.

"Come on, Josephine!" said Mrs Edwards, smiling and waving her hand.

I looked questioningly at Mrs White, who bent to her book and said, "Okay. Turn to page eighteen."

"Josephine!" called Mrs Edwards. "Come on!"

Without looking up, my teacher said, "Hurry up, child!"

I jumped up and almost ran to the door. Mrs Edwards put her arm around me, patting me solidly on the back as we walked down the corridor, saying, "Poor little Josephine Chin."

After that I always went with Mrs Edwards, who would say wonderful things like, "Don't forget Josephine, she's my best helper, you know!" or "Come on, Josephine! You know you're always one of my team!"

And in the many dark days of Standard Two and Three, the short, squat figure bursting down the corridor would bring the most brilliant light to my day. For a few hours, I would be the helpful, smart, happy Josephine. And nothing could take that away.

And as if she hadn't already done enough, Mrs Edwards found me a new joy, a new escape. For she started a choir that year, and when each teacher was asked to test us and submit names, and mine, of course was not on the list, Mrs Edwards came to our room, bringing Sister Angelica with her.

Beaming, she said, "Sister wanted to hear the girls you picked, Miss."

Mrs White smiled, called forth her choir, and they sang a verse of our morning hymn; Sister and teacher and Mrs Edwards were all smiles.

"Thank you, Miss. They sound great!"

As they turned to walk away, Mrs Edwards turned back as if she'd forgotten something. Pursing her lips and putting her finger to them she said, "I just wondered something, Miss. You know Josephine has such a lovely voice when she's talking, I wonder if we might hear her sing?"

Mrs Edwards looked at Sister Angelica, who nodded.

"Stand up, child," said Sister Angelica in her cold, horrible voice. "Let's hear the first verse of this morning's hymn."

What on earth was Mrs Edwards doing? I could barely breathe in front of Sister Angelica! How could I sing? I stood as ordered, my legs feeling like jello. I felt to vomit. I opened my mouth and nothing came out. Sister Angelica's harsh, grey eyebrow lifted. I coughed. Mrs Edwards smiled and nodded at me. I opened my mouth again. Nothing.

Sister Angelica turned away. "Sit down, child," she said, as she began walking off.

As I bent my head and started to sit, I saw the gleeful look on Mrs White's face, and Mrs Edwards, still hesitating at the door even though Sister was a few steps down the corridor, was smiling at me – a different smile, though. It reminded me of another time. Another voice. Another angel.

And I stood up straight, and started to sing.

And Sister Angelica stopped, turned around, slowly, mouth agape, and for once I stared at her and was not afraid. Mrs Edwards looked at Sister and smiled before she bent to her book of names of choir singers and scribbled in it. She looked up at me with a smile.

"Thank you, Josephine. See you at practice!" Then she turned to my teacher. "Thank you, Miss."

It was the first time I saw Mrs Edwards not smiling. And Mrs White bent her head, suddenly absorbed in the books before her.

So between the outings and choir with Mrs Edwards, I found an ease to tide me through the other times, and survived again, another year.

Though the first day of school had always been a dreaded day for me, the first day of the new term for Standard Three made me shudder even more than usual. It was one of those days when you start out with a weight in your stomach that tells you today is going to be a really bad day. When I got to school, realizing that I was not the first today, but second to horrible Wendy, my dread redefined itself. For she was sitting in the seat that had been assigned to me the previous term, and I knew enough of Mrs White's tactics not to go to a new seat. So I walked to the desk and put my bag on the floor, next to hers.

"Doh put that there," Wendy said, "that is Caroline seat." Caroline was her best friend, and one of the ringleaders in my constant circle of ridicule.

"I sit here," I said.

"Not again," she answered.

I left my bag and walked out to the corridor. Then I heard Wendy laughing.

"Where you get that old bag from?" she said.

I had found this sort of leather grip in a cupboard at home, some relic from one of my older sisters. It was faded brown and dusty and opened like a briefcase, but I loved it. I'd taken it down and transferred my newly covered books from my new bag into this one. No amount of teasing from Cleo deterred me, for I was accustomed to this from her and I couldn't care less what she thought. When she ran and told my mother, who ordered me to "put that stupid, dusty bag away", I hissed at her. But when she walked off, in triumph, the books went back in. Because I was always last to get to the car, and everyone was stressed out to reach to school on time, nobody saw when I hustled into the car, pulling the grip behind me. Of course when my mother did see the grip she could do nothing as we had already got to school, so, amidst the laughter of my sister and my mother's steupses, I walked down the school corridor, dragging my beloved grip.

I had ignored everyone at home, so now I ignored Wendy as she laughed behind me.

The school started filling up with the noise of hundreds of girls returning to find their friends after the holidays. Then a strange quiet behind me made me turn around. A small circle of girls stood at the front of the class, pointing and laughing at something in the middle. I walked towards the circle, not surprised to see that my bag was the object of their delight.

"Yuh old uncle dead and leave this bag for yuh or what?" jeered Caroline.

Raucous laughter.

"Give me my bag!" I said, pushing through the circle and picking up the grip. I jammed it against the desk where I had left it and stood in front of it.

"That is Caroline seat I tell you," said Wendy, bending to pick up my bag.

"Doh touch that, girl!" shouted Caroline. "Yuh might ketch something!"

Laughter.

Wendy grinned, picked up her bag and swung it into mine, sending the grip skidding across the floor, its unfaithful clasp opening and spilling out my books. The circle howled with laughter. I could see girls from other classes coming over, grinning; while behind us stood most of my class, looking on uncomfortably.

I could feel tears coming, so I spun around and marched out of the class, not knowing where I was going, only hearing someone say, "Oh look! She going to tell she mamee." And more laughter.

I walked across the courtyard, straight past my mother's classroom and into the class next door. Mrs Singh's. The most feared teacher in our school.

"What's the matter, Josephine?" Mrs Singh got off her chair and walked towards me. Now the tears came, and I covered my face with my hands to hide them. Mrs Singh put her arm around me.

"What's wrong? Is someone troubling you?"

I nodded without moving my hands.

"Come," she said.

Still with her arm around me, she moved briskly towards my classroom. I wiped my face, looked up, saw my mother's shocked expression as we walked briskly past her room; saw a handful of girls scamper from the door of my class and run inside.

By the time we got to my class, my bag was packed and returned to its place, and Wendy and Caroline sat at another desk, reading their textbooks. As we entered, everyone jumped up, calling loudly, "Good morning, Miss!"

"Good morning, girls," she answered. "Josephine seems to be having some trouble today. What is going on here?"

Silence.

Mrs Singh turned to me. "Who is it, Josephine?"

I looked at Wendy and Caroline, whose eyes pleaded with me. I lifted my arm and pointed them out. Mrs Singh marched up to them and dragged them into a standing position by their shirt collars. She shook them.

"What is this nonsense?" she shouted.

They bent their heads and she shook them again.

"I don't know what you did Josephine this morning, but it better not happen again!" She shook them once more. "Do you hear me?"

"Yes, Miss," they mumbled.

"Look at me!" she said. They looked up. "This better not happen again or you will have me to deal with!"

"Yes, Miss."

"Apologize to Josephine."

"Sorry, Josephine."

Mrs Singh let them go. She turned to the class and said, "If I hear any more of this nonsense, you will have me to deal with. Understood?"

"Yes, Miss."

Then she turned to me. "Josephine," she said, "you come and tell me if anyone is troubling you ever again. Okay?"

I nodded.

When Mrs Singh walked out and I walked to my desk and sat down, the quiet was so loud, it echoed in my ears.

And though the teasing didn't completely stop, it became much less. More so, there was a new knowledge on my part, an understanding in some distant part of my being that, despite everything, somehow I was supported, looked out for; an understanding that I had learnt not just to survive, but to have laughter in easy, ready supply. Being the youngest at home, with teasing sisters like Mary and Angie and grumpy ones like Cleo, and kind ones like Bernie, I would have been flattened had I not had this understanding, for our mother was too tired and stressed to know the half of what we did, much more come to my rescue. With some inner wisdom, I kept the knowledge from valuable lessons learnt along the way well hidden in the folds of my memory, giving me a tool for survival.

And because of these angels who had rescued me, my spirit got to peep out every so often, despite the fact that I knew of the Devil's ability to hide in it; for these angels had shown me that, sometimes, the spirit can be a good thing.

Finally!

It was only in Standard Five that the teasing truly stopped, in part because of this change in my attitude, in part because the posse of teasers considered themselves now too mature for such childish things, and mainly because our teacher, Mrs Bellesmythe, would not allow it. She showed no favouritism, and was actually indebted to my mother who had taught her niece the previous year, and who had encouraged the other girls to play with the niece when my mother saw that she was being ignored.

So my last two years at this school weren't so bad. In addition to all this, I had some rank because, thanks to Mrs Edwards, I was in both the school choir and choral speaking, and so enjoyed the privilege of such treats as getting to leave class and performing at shows. My earlier tormentors had no time for me, having discovered a new fascination: boys. So now I found people I had never spoken to in my five years here, coming up to me, and I had new friends, though they were not like Maria and Antonia. The whole class became one, as former pets discovered they ranked lower and the tortured now found themselves encouraged. Only the Wendy and Caroline posse continued to ignore me. Generally, I was on talking basis with some and more friendly with others.

Until the day of the calypso competition.

For the first time, our school had a fantastic Carnival celebration when we were in Standard Five. This was due to the presence of a vibrant committee, headed by Mrs Edwards. Sister Angelica was talked into it, for this committee held firepower – they raised funds for the school.

We were told that, as Standard Fives, we would be allowed to help organize the show and perform calypsoes, and that this was a trial run; whether it would become annual would depend on us, and on our ability to reject the darkness and remember the whiteness of our souls, even at this time of sin called 'Carnival'.

Somehow, Sister Angelica was persuaded to "borrow" a drummer from the Boys' RC School, and the girls who were in the know pushed for Derek Leechung. The whisper that he was coming to our school rippled like a wave and we pulsed with barely controlled excitement. Those of us who didn't know him were given the full description of his Chinese eyes, curly hair, bronze complexion, and his reputed dimples. Just the mention of his name made many swoon, and of course many bragged that they'd been kissed by him. Had Sister Angelica known what conversations were spurred by the mention of his name, she not only would have abandoned the whole calypso idea, but sent us all down on our knees for an entire day to beg forgiveness for our sinful thoughts.

Of course Derek didn't come to practise, that would have been too much distraction, so some girl was chosen to beat the desk while we ran through our songs in the evenings; her poor attempts made us anticipate all the more the feast that awaited us on Calypso Competition Day.

The day of the competition we were antsy. A boy had never entered our school before, much less a gorgeous boy. We didn't even know when he came, for we had to stay in our classrooms until it was exactly time for the show to start and Derek was kept hidden until calypso time. It seemed as though the clock would never say ten o'clock.

At the blessed hour, the bell rang. We were summoned to the hall, and we looked and looked, but all we could see was the ghostly figure of Sister Angelica, standing in the middle of the stage, in front of the mike. Our hearts dropped. And then her cold voice echoed throughout the school.

"Good morning, girls," she said.

We answered as best we could, the disappointment heavy inside us.

"Well," she said, "I hope you'll have more energy than that for the Calypso Competition."

And then, from the side of the stage, we could see a teacher ushering on someone and, yes! It was him! Our hearts rose collectively and our stifled excitement emerged as a huge sigh. Energy sizzled through the hall like Carnival heat itself, and then Sister Angelica's voice came on again, reminding us of where we were, who we were.

"If you are going to behave like fishwives, I will stop this show right now!" she threatened.

We held our breaths, knowing that even breathing could give us away. Sister Angelica went on to remind us to be like Jesus, clean in mind, body and spirit, not to let the music of Carnival bring the Devil into our souls and, finally, not to commit the sin of lust, for the boy from the Boys' RC was nothing more than a little drummer boy, come to serenade Jesus today.

The school became quiet – not that we believed her, but we wanted nothing to stop this show. Sister smiled, wondering at the power of her little speech. Then she said, "Very well. Now stand for a prayer and the anthem."

We prayed and sang hard, each of the two thousand voices trying to reach and impress the ears of Derek Leechung, buoyed by the sight of him standing on the stage, singing with us. At the end, the collective sigh could not be stifled. We were all in love.

And then it was time to line up, group by group, for the competition. I had been asked by Carrie Moore to sing with her group. 'Give Hasely Crawford the Gold!' – that was our song. We were the last contestants, shaking and jumping backstage as other girls came off, raving about how good Derek was, about how he smiled with them. From the side of the stage we could, by stretching our necks a little, see part of the top of his drum, with one hand resting on it, tapping, tapping, waiting to bring us emancipation. We pinched each other and muffled screams.

Then we heard Mrs White saying, "And, finally, from Standard Five A, The Olympiads! With their song, 'Give Hasely Crawford the Gold!' "

Excited by the cheers we filed onto the stage, the bolder among us looking Derek in the eye and smiling. I looked at my sneakers, losing suddenly all my Roger Johnish attitude; I was, anyway, out of practice, since Roger John was now no longer an ice-cream boy but a teenager, forever lost to me.

Somehow we remembered our words and our dance, singing the praises of Hasely Crawford, our first and so far only Olympic gold medallist, more proud of him because he'd beaten Jamaica's Don Quarry who, we sang, had "the bronze to hold".

We were good and we knew it. And Derek Leechung was grinning and beating and shaking his head along with us. The screams when we were done could not be stopped. We grinned. We patted Carrie on the back and stood there, foolish with our glory, until Mrs White had to shoo us off the stage. As we filed past Derek Leechung, who was grinning and nodding, I was brave enough now, after our triumphant stage debut, to look at him; I saw his grin change into a smile.

"Hello," he said to me.

My heart jumped up into my neck. I blushed and focused on my sneakers, hating Roger John for my dotishness. I walked quickly past. And as I got off stage, a group of wide-opened eyes and mouths met me.

Because it was me.

Me!

Teased and taunted, wetting-herself Josephine Chin, who only the cutest boy in Boy School had just said hello to.

Part Two

Between Heaven and Hell

"Temptation, Infatuation, Confession … Life Progression"

Josephine Chin

Temptation, Infatuation, Confession …

∞∞∞

For all my 'fresh-little-girlness' and attention-getting from only *the* biggest heart-throb around, I was as innocent and unknowing as they come. My ignorance about sex and the male species was, even back then, shocking. But this situation was soon to be rectified, for on my first day at Convent I was put to sit by a girl called Cavelle Gray.

I went into Convent with the distaste for school bred from seven years at St Maria's, but a batch of young teachers saved me from myself. They were not angels like Mrs Simmons and Mrs Edwards and Mrs Singh. These were worldly-wise women enjoying the independence of their first job; filled with belief in their ability to make a difference through teaching, they marched to no one's drum but their own.

For the first time, teachers tapped into me and found an intelligence that I myself was unaware of. Now, too, the Chin name worked for me; many of these young teachers had been taught by my mother, others were friends of my older sisters, and these teachers adored me. They weathered my low self-esteem and wooed me out of feigned nonchalance into my natural state of curiosity. To reward their kindness, I showed my gratitude by excelling in the subjects they taught: history, geography, literature, English language. My stories became well-known pieces of class study and analysis, and this credit given to my work filled me with awe of my own abilities. Our music teacher, grumpy to everyone else, showed patience and persistence with me until she pulled from me, not just the singing voice that Mrs Edwards had found, but also a musical ear that she trained until I could both read and write music.

Yet being teachers' pet for the first time did not make me pompous. I had for too long been the victim of the adverse effects of teacher favouritism. Instead, I silently pledged that, if ever I became a teacher, I would recognize the power to build or crush, for I knew now that being teachers' beloved was as dangerous as being teachers' bobolee. Throughout this self-esteem building exercise, there were many old teachers who knew and hated the Chin name. One in particular, Miss Rajnath, our math teacher, rolled her eyes to heaven as if imploring help as she said, on seeing me, "Oh dear, another Chin."

All I could think, as I looked at the short, squat black woman glaring at me with goggly eyes from behind her glasses, was to wonder whatever made her believe her help would come from heaven; all I could see were her many warts, and the image of a toad made itself most present in my mind, so that I must have gaped or giggled enough to make her, before the class was done, find an excuse to have me kneel beside my seat.

As I knelt, expecting the laughs and giggles of old, surprised that there were none, surprised that Miss Rajnath, looking at the class expectantly, got only bored and angry looks in return, I felt a relief so immense I sighed aloud. At the end of class our teacher, realizing her mistake, pretended to be sorry for me and proceeded to give me a lecture which, she said, was designed to break the Chin bad luck with math. She knew of course that I did not believe her; I have never been able to hide dislike, and dislike was all I felt for her. So we went into guerilla tactics after that, she finding every opportunity to lament on the Chin deficiency in math, and me failing every single test she ever gave. So well did Miss Rajnath do her job that to this day the mere sight of numbers, or the idea of figuring out something mathematical, gives me an instant headache and I get thoroughly confused.

Never again did school have the power over me that it had had in primary school, for as Miss Rajnath left and I got up, dusting my knees, I met the eye of our next teacher coming in for her class, and by the time I had sat down and taken out my literature book, she was saying, "Josephine, please read for us today, yours is the only voice to bring us back to peace this evening."

Of course she said it loudly enough for Miss Rajnath, walking down the corridor, to hear, sending, as she did so, many more messages than I imagined.

Now, too, our classes were filled with girls who did not know me from before, who did not know my mother was a teacher at St Maria's, had, in fact, never heard of St Maria's, and I found myself being befriended. I could not escape these new girls who stared at me in fascination, looking from my kinky hair to my slanted eyes, and saying: "Chin? Yuh name is Chin? Yuh sure?"

And the curiosity grew when they saw my older sister, Cleo, with dead straight hair, and some were bold enough to ask what all the others wanted to know, "All yuh have the same father and mother?"

Yet teachers and older people kept seeing me as a Chin even while I wished they would not.

"All of you have the same face," they would say, and I would shudder to think I looked like Cleo, whose nose, especially on one of her many angry days, spanned a great deal of her face. Grudgingly, I did see the resemblance, but only in photos, perhaps myself blinded by those minor variations of hair and colour that make so much difference.

The white girls especially asked about our parents, but they gravitated to me nonetheless, for many of them had been taught by my older sister, Angie, in the private primary school where she had worked before going to UWI. And the East Indians came, saying, "You have a real nice complexion," and, "How you so fair?" While from my own kind, the Africans and Chinese, I got the greatest snobbery.

But a far more exciting development than all this was taking place in my world of learning. Let me return to Cavelle Gray.

There was nothing innocent about Cavelle Gray. She had breasts and hips envied by all. When she put her head on her desk and moaned every twenty-eight days, we envied her her period pains. She had shaven legs and plucked eyebrows – all this, and she wasn't even white! For white girls, we knew, did these things, had these things before us, after all, they were white, and everyone knew they weren't very bright, or didn't have to study school because their parents had businesses to put them into after they graduated, and everyone knew that white girls could fool around without getting bad reputations at school, at least, not among people we knew, so white girls with these attitudes and attributes were expected; but this Cavelle was a different story. And to go with her voluptuousness she had a mouth like a sewer. I learnt many inventive curse words. Her mind, she used to say, lay in the gutter while she was at school, but I swear her mind sat next to me, for the stories with which she regaled me, of what she did and did not do with her boyfriend, reminded me of what my mother termed "behaving like a gutter rat".

Cavelle told me she'd been having sex since she was nine, how she loved to French kiss till her tongue hurt, and how she washed her face with sperm every week to keep away pimples. Most of these words were ones I'd heard, but didn't know what the actions involved, but of course my wide-eyed innocence became too boring even to me, and so I lied: I'd been to the beach this weekend and been kissed by a cute boy in the water;

I'd gone to a fete (*ha!*) with my older sister and sneaked off with some nineteen-year-old boy. I lied. I lied. I lied. Looking back now, I wonder how many of Cavelle's stories were actually true!

Thus began my sex education.

Even growing up with five older sisters, I learnt more about sex from Cavelle in that first term at Covent than I'd ever done at home. At least, I learnt the terms; what I didn't know, I pretended I did, rolling my eyes, giggling, and generally giving the appropriate action that made me appear knowledgeable enough to be Cavelle's confidante. Words like "blow job" and "condom" were added to my vocabulary, and in the evenings, when I looked them up and found most were not in the dictionary, the idea that I was learning about such forbidden deeds made them more spicy.

One day she lifted her skirt to show me some blue and black marks on her legs.

"Oh my God!" I said, horrified, "It hurt?"

Cavelle's head rolled back and she screamed with laughter. "God, Josephine!" she said, grinning. "Yuh doh know what a hickey is?"

"Of course I do!" I snapped. Of course, I did not. "But those – they must have hurt, look how big and black they are."

Always one to seize the moment, Cavelle dropped her skirt and lowered her tone.

"Yes, yuh right, it hurt, oui," she said. Then, turning to me and grinning in conspiracy, "But I liked it!"

I quickly masked my shock and grinned too, nodding, as if understanding. For the rest of the day, Cavelle walked around with a slight limp, winking at me when she told the other girls she couldn't play rounders that day.

I feared and envied her. Her ruthlessness, her passion, seemed to reach some fertile soil inside me and dared it to sprout, but each time I thought of it sprouting little leaves, the image of my mother's face would wilt them quicker than drought. Like a little devil, Cavelle tempted and teased, tested and tried, knowing I wouldn't bite the apple and making me wish I would.

We all treated her with a kind of amusement and jealousy at the same time. We wondered, when we saw her talking and giggling with the white girls, what trysts she had been on that were too much to tell us. She was crazy! We hated and loved her, and her energy was so all-consuming that, when she left at the end of the first term to return to the States with her American mother – who, she said, couldn't make it in Trinidad with this new Trini man – the space on the seat next to me filled the whole class with a void. As ridiculous and unbelievable as Cavelle was with, as Sister Ruth put it, her "unstable family life", we all wanted to be her.

Hickeys on the leg! Ha! She had us all fooled for years!

What innocence Cavelle had left me with was soon to be taken away by Mr Harris that August, when my mother took Cleo and me to Tobago for a holiday.

Angie

I tiptoed into the room their scandalous laughter was coming from. Angie and Mel, her best friend, were lying on the bed, laughing so much the bed rocked hard. Mel's legs were up in the air kicking desperately, as she cackled with laughter. I stood by the door grinning.

"Ay, Jo," gasped Angie, looking up and seeing me.

"Wha's the joke?" I asked.

"Nothing," said Angie sitting up, grinning as she wiped the tears off her face, "just something Mel was saying. Come nah."

"Stop that noise!" shouted my mother from the kitchen.

"Sorry, Mum," said Angie as she poked Mel to stop her from laughing.

Unlike Cleo, Angie never made me feel like a pesky little sister, even though she was older than Cleo. Sometimes Angie was like a big child herself; making up stupid stories for our nieces and nephews and having us play all kinds of silly games.

Now, I sat on the bed with her and Mel, grinning too.

"Oh, God," said Mel wiping her face, "like I can't stop laughing, Ang." She turned on her side, held her belly and squealed loudly.

Angie started to laugh again. "Panting like a frighten pig, you say?" she screamed, and choked, trying to hold the laughter that would not stop, and then covered her mouth as she slapped Mel on the back.

"Angie!" called Mummy from the kitchen.

"Sorry, Mum!" said Angie, still grinning.

And then we got quiet. We could hear our mother's footsteps coming down the corridor. Angie and Mel stopped grinning and looked expectantly at the doorway.

"All yuh don't find I have enough to do without all this noise?" snapped our mother. Standing in the doorway with a pot spoon in one hand and a kitchen towel in the other, she glared at us.

"Sorry, Mum."

"Sorry, Auntie."

"Stop that foolishness and get ready to wash the wares when I done cook, Angie."

"Yes, Mum," said Angie, looking contrite.

"Wha's that?" I whispered, pointing to a tiny packet that peeked out from under Mel when she grinned and rolled over as Mummy walked off.

They looked at each other and burst out laughing again. Mel pulled the packet out from under her and I could see tiny white tablets on the other side of it.

"She wouldn't tell?" Mel asked Angie, her eyes opening wide.

Angie shook her head, squeezing back tears. "Yuh won't tell, ent, Jo?"

"Tell what?" I asked.

"About this, Josephine!" snapped Mel, waving the packet in front of me.

"What it is?"

Mel rolled her eyes and looked at Angie. They both got serious now. They sat up at the same time and stared at me.

"You have to promise you won't tell," said Angie.

"Okay," I said, "okay. I won't tell."

"Is tablets," said Mel.

"I could see that," I said. "What happen? You sick?"

Mel pursed her lips to hide a smile. Angie snorted and glanced at Mel. "Yuh could say that," she said, grinning, as Mel poked her in the side.

"With what?" I said. "How you could be sick and you laughing about it so? Who sick, you or Angie?"

"Nobody sick, Jo," said Angie, "is tablets for something else."

"What?" I said, looking from one to the other, fed up with the suspense.

"Promise, Josephine," said Angie, getting all grown up on me suddenly.

"I promise," I said again.

"Is for sex," said Angie.

"Sex?" I said, my eyes opened wide.

"Yes. Sex," said Mel, watching me hard.

"Why?" I said, staring at Angie.

"So she ... I mean ... somebody, won't get pregnant."

"Oh," I said, recalling my Cavelle conversations and trying to sound grown up.

"Yes," said Mel, "is so whoever use it doh get pregnant."

"Yuh know what sex is, right, Josephine?"

For a minute, I almost nodded and pretended, like I was so accustomed doing, but then I shook my head, no.

"No?" said Mel in shock.

I cut my eyes at her.

"Is when a man and woman go to bed together and the man lie on top the woman," said Angie, blushing.

"Oh," I say. Was that all?

"And?" said Mel, poking Angie.

"And the man puts his ... am ... thing ... in the woman's ... you know ..."

"Where?" I said. "What?"

Angie points at my crotch.

"What?" I said, jumping up and covering myself there. "Oh gad!"

Mel and Angie burst out laughing and pull me onto the bed.

Since the previous year, my mother had started taking Cleo and me on holiday every August vacation, and this year we stayed at an Inn on the now exclusive Pigeon Point beach in Tobago. The owner, Mr Harris, an old white man, took a great liking to us and would often come to sit with us at dinner. I did not like him, but my mother, thoroughly colonized, was awed by the attentions of a white man and pushed us to talk and be friendly.

There were lots of other children at the Inn and sometimes I played with them since, holiday or not, Cleo was still Cleo. Once another girl and I were playing on the beach and Mr Harris suddenly appeared. Smiling, he came over to talk to us. A strange feeling came over me, but I was too naïve to know it was fear. I understood fear of Sister Angelica, or fear of a horror movie, but this smiling, white face had no bearing on fear. And then my friend's mother appeared; clapping her hands she loudly called her daughter over to her. I took the opportunity to run.

The following day, we were playing a rowdy game of catch in one of the downstairs corridors. A door opened and Mr Harris's head popped out. Scared that we'd been too loud, I looked at him, but he smiled and beckoned me with his finger. The other children ran off, continuing the game, unaware that I'd taken tentative steps towards his door.

"Come in, come in, Josephine," he said, smiling.

Uncertainly, I entered.

"This is where I live," he said, his hand making an expansive move and landing on my shoulder. Behind me, he walked forward, his hand pressing my shoulder so that I followed his guidance, even as I led the way, and I found myself suddenly facing a gigantic bed.

"This is my bed," he said. His hand slid from my shoulder and brushed the front of my blouse.

I felt uncomfortable and totally, totally confused as to why I would be interested in his bed. Then Mr Harris was standing in front me, smiling.

"Would you like to feel it?" he asked. "It's very comfortable."

My breasts hurt. Looking down, I was surprised to see my top unbuttoned and chubby fingers squeezing my nipples. We stood facing each other, me seeing only the enormous bed behind him, still wondering why he brought me here, too stupid to scream or run or something, while he smiled and squeezed my nipples hard. A memory opened and I vaguely recalled Angie's words about sex and then, as would happen many, many times in my life, I was rescued by my angels, the first time I would feel the power of unseen angels, as I said, calmly, the right words to set me free.

"No. If I doh go now, somebody will come looking for me."

He stopped so quickly that I did not know I was yet released. But I saw the look in his eyes had changed, and I recognized fear in them. Still unsure of what was going on, still too stupid to run, I turned and started walking back to the door, buttoning my shirt as I did.

"You won't say anything? You won't tell anyone?" he pleaded behind me.

"No," I said, as I got to the door.

From behind me, he reached and opened the door, his hand touching mine as he did.

And then I ran.

And I never did.

Tell anyone.

Until a year later, when my mother came, showing me a small article in the newspaper: *Sunset Beach Inn Folds*.

"What a pity," she lamented, "such a nice place. Such a nice man. Poor fella."

"It good!" I blurted.

"What happen to you?" she said.

And then I told her. Told her about Mr Harris. The nice man. I didn't cry. I was just angry. Grown up enough over the year to know what I had been was molested. I knew enough now to be angry.

My mother's mouth formed an 'O', her eyes rolled to heaven, her hands clasped her face.

"Why you didn't tell me?" she asked.

"Because … I doh know. I forgot."

She made clucking noises, shaking her head.

"Besides," I continued, feeling the pain I should have felt then, "I never used to want to talk to him. Is you always pushing us. 'Talk to the man, nah.' 'Doh be rude, nah.'" I spat this last part at her.

Feeling my anger now, knowing it was right, my mother retaliated.

"Well!" she huffed, walking off. "I was just being nice!"

"Nice?" I shouted. "He didn't deserve 'nice'! He's a nastiness! It good for him! It damn good!"

I was sobbing now, my right nipple throbbed with angry remembrance. I had never used these words with my mother, but I did not care now. I was angrier than I had ever known myself to be. And then, like some far away echo, my mother's voice from the corridor.

"You sure? Yuh sure he do that, child?"

I stared at her.

And then I got up and went outside.

To the swing.

Desperately needing to be rocked.

The comb fought its way through my hair. By the time it was pulled through, my eyes were watering and my scalp was sore. I pressed my bottom to the ground, squeezed my eyes tight, and inhaled as the comb began its trek at the top of my head again.

"Ow!" I yelled, as it bounced, reversed and slammed into a huge knot. "Ow! That hurting!"

"I doh know why you doh comb this hair!" snapped my mother, manoeuvring her weapon until it grasped the knot and yanked through. Steupsing, she pulled the knotted hair from the comb and dropped it into my lap like a grenade. My hand went to the spot on my head, throbbing with pain, and I rubbed it, sniffling as I did so.

The comb rapped my hand. "Move yuh hand," said my mother. "I doh have whole day to sit down with this mess you know."

My shoulders hunched and I held my breath as the comb took up position again. And then the phone rang.

"Mummy!" called my eldest sister, Jessie, from inside, "Phone for you."

I exhaled, both hands going automatically to my head and rubbing it. Rubbing it. Mummy pressed her hand down onto my back and lifted her leg over it. Getting up, she said, "Doh rumple up what I do there, eh."

I pressed my back into the chair behind me and closed my eyes, continuing to rub my head. Then I heard a whisper in the corridor.

"Jo! Jo!"

I sat up, opened my eyes.

"Come!" mouthed Jessie.

Wiping my face, I got up and followed her into the bedroom. She walked to the dressing table and stood behind the chair, grinning, holding a pair of scissors in her hand.

My eyes opened wide. "You crazy?" I said.

"Shh!" Jessie put her finger to her lips. "Come!" she whispered. "Quick!" She patted the back of the chair. I walked to it and sat down, gaping at Jessie in the mirror.

"Mummy will kill me!" I said.

"You really want to go back and sit down there?"

I shook my head no.

"Good." The scissors lifted.

"Wait!" I grabbed her hand. "Oh gawd! Mummy will quarrel!"

"So?" said Jessie, "What she will do? Make you stick it back on?"

I let go of her hand, still doubtfully looking at her in the mirror.

"Well …" I said.

"Look. She does quarrel anyway?"

I nodded.

"Well, at least when she quarrel you doh have to sit back down for that torture again. Right?" I nodded again.

Her hand picked up, from the still tangled half of head, a mass of hair, scissors poised, then, seriously, she said, "What to do, Josephine? Cut it or not?"

I nodded.

Jessie

"Well? How I looking?" I asked, twisting and turning in front of the mirror.

"Very nice, Josie," said Jessie, smiling behind me.

"You sure?"

She nodded.

"Okay. Well, let me just go and show Miss Carmen," I said.

Jessie looked at her watch, "We doh have much time."

"Doh worry, I won't take long."

I ran from the room, down the corridor, and started calling Miss Carmen.

"Josephine, stop making all that noise!" said my mother from her room.

I slowed my steps and walked to Mummy's room, poked my head through the door.

"How I looking, Mom?" I asked shyly.

My mother looked up from a mountain of copybooks on her desk. "Good," she said, glancing at me and then resuming marking her books. "Tell Jessie not to come back too late."

"Okay," I said, as I backed out of the room.

By the time I reached the back door, I was calling Miss Carmen again, so that she was waiting and smiling by her window when I reached the fence.

"Well?" I said to her, smiling as I turned all the way around slowly.

"Yuh looking sharp, man, Josephine. Where yuh going dress up so?"

"Jessie taking me to the Library. Me and some other girls going to sing a Teddy Bear song. And she get this costume make for me. And we have to do a dance too. Yuh want to see it?"

I was just stooping into position when I heard Jessie call me.

"Oh! Sorry, Miss Carmen. I have to go now!" I said, running back to the house.

"Okay, Josephine! Have fun!" called Miss Carmen behind me.

I was so excited, I chatted all the way, but when I got to the Library and saw all the people, I grabbed Jessie's hand.

"Jessie!" I whispered, pulling on her hand for her to stop walking.

"What?" she said, standing in front of me.

"I … can't do this …"

"Why?"

"So much people. I change my mind."

"Oh, Josephine," said Jessie, stooping in front me, "yuh frighten?"

I nodded.

"Why?"

I shrugged.

"Is all people you know," said Jessie.

I stared at her doubtfully.

She turned. "Look, see there?" she said, pointing. "Look, Claudine and Anna and Stella, all my friends. The same people you talk with every Saturday when you come."

"So?" I said. "What about them?" I pointed to a group on the other side of the room, "And them?"

"That is just their friends and family, nobody special," said Jessie.

"You sure?"

"Yes, Josephine, I sure," said Jessie. Turning me around to face the makeshift wall, she whispered in my ear, "And besides, the other teddy bears waiting for the star teddy bear to sing and dance."

I turned to face her, grinning. "I am the star teddy bear?" I asked.

Jessie frowned. "So you doh know that?" she said.

I shook my head.

"Annie and Susan and Lisa and Karen, all yuh friends waiting behind there for you."

Jessie stood up, walked in front of me, held out her hand. "So then, you coming or what?"

I reached for her hand and nodded, grinning again.

Only when I felt the scissors waver did I look up. Up and across. Across to the door. My body stiffened. Mummy stood in the doorway, her face a terrible mask of disbelief and anger. I looked away quickly. And then I could feel Jessie's hand press into my shoulder, and move with sureness into my hair. The scissors lifted again; its snip echoed throughout the room. I did not dare look at my sister in the mirror.

And then Mummy reached the dressing table, pounded it with her fist, shouting, "What yuh doing? What yuh doing to the child head?"

Jessie ignored her and continued snipping. Mummy slapped at Jessie's hand, shouting,

"What yuh do that for?"

Jessie pulled her hand away, looked Mummy straight in the eyes.

"Saving her from more torture. That's what I doing," she said.

I trembled between them, looking from one to the other, jumping when my mother's eyes dug into me. "Yuh looking like a little nigger now!" she spat.

With trembling legs I got up off the chair, walking slowly out of the room, dreading, with every step, my mother's fire, my only comfort being Jessie, who was home for the weekend; if there was one soldier I could depend on, it was Jessie. But fate was with me that day. As I got to the back door and poked my head out, I saw Aunty Lyn, my brother's wife, coming in with her niece,

Jean, who I'd been friends with since Standard Five, and – miracle! Jean's hair was, of all things, cut into an Afro. We stared at each other and Aunty Lyn said, "Josephine! It look good!"

My mother looked up at me with one of her wry smiles. Aunty Lyn turned to her.

"Aunty Nora, you must be glad, eh? No more untangling that hair every evening!"

My mother looked at Aunty Lyn, decided her smile was genuine, and then looked back at me, as if in sudden realization. She really smiled now. And then she nodded.

"Yes," she said, "yes. Is true."

But it was the impact that this haircut had on my social life at school that was the big surprise. That, and my father's reaction.

Monday morning, and there was the usual posse that had ignored me before, the "hard-headed Negroes" as my mother had referred to them, gaping at me as I walked in through the school gate. Somehow, the word got around that I was 'cool', and by breaktime some of my old arch-enemies from St Maria's started, hesitantly at first, then more boldly, coming to talk to me, while the Indians and whites who had first befriended me kept giving me puzzled looks and watery smiles, until, eventually, someone asked, "What yuh do yuh hair?"

By lunchtime I was enjoying the surprised looks in people's eyes, and in the evening, when I went as usual across to the Promenade with Jean and Carol and noticed the Presentation and Benedict's boys, who came every day to see what Convent had to offer, nudging each other and staring at me, I couldn't help but grin. It was like Derek Leechung all over again, only this time I recognized my power.

When I left school that day I was floating on a cloud. And when the dreaded hour came, the hour that I usually spent on the floor between my mother's knees, and my heart tightened and then slowly relaxed as I remembered, and I found myself with an hour of free, blissful time, I was truly in heaven. Swinging high and singing and free. And then my father came two days later and shot me down from the apex of joy.

Daddy

My father prided himself on thrift and a sense of humour. His favourite saying, "Good ting no cheap and cheap ting no good", left one to wonder whether he himself was any good, as he hunted the length of High Street for bargains and would walk all the way back to the top store if something was five cents cheaper there. His repertoire of corny jokes would bring us to tears, and though he never told a good joke, he always told a joke good.

Daddy's tomato red Volkswagen pulling up to our gate filled me with joy and fear, as I struggled to rebuff his charm and remain in constant allegiance to my mother, even while the mere sight of him filled me with accountable joy. For many years, before I trusted his friendship, I would, as instructed, march outside with hand extended, reciting my well-learnt litany of financial woes.

"Dad, I need money for shoes, and school, and I have no clothes."

And always he sought to break my defences with a smile. Arms outstretched, he would reply, "So, Josephine, you not going to give yuh father a kiss?"

And I would move stiffly into the embrace, brush his grizzly cheek with a cold kiss and step back, out of the arms that asked for more, acutely aware of my mother's watchful eyes that controlled me from the living room window.

Even when outings to the cinema to see his favourite Shaolin Masters turned out to be fun, even when I laughed at his jokes and his teasing as he dug into each pocket before he could find money to give me, even then, I held on fervently to the wife-abuser, child-abandoner knowledge engrained in me, and refused to let him in.

Until the August I turned thirteen.

That vacation, I came to see my father, and when I did, he showed me life.

In the first week of that vacation my father came to take Cleo and me to the bank to open a fixed deposit account for us. I remember the bank being crowded and the line inching slowly forward. We finally got to the counter and faced a young, pompous teller.

"Good day to you, sir," said my father. "I'm here to open a fixed deposit for my daughters."

Grandly, my father pulled a large, white envelope from his pocket and placed it on the counter.

The young man took the envelope, pulled out the curled, creased notes of the working man and counted them out. He looked up, bored, unimpressed, and said, "Will that be all?"

My sister's nose flared. Like my mother, I fumed but said nothing. My father smiled and nodded.

The young man took the envelope, walked to a desk at the back, picked up the telephone and adjusted himself into a pose that promised a hearty conversation. I looked at the clock on the wall. Five minutes passed. We looked at our father, waiting for him to say or do something; still he smiled. The clock's hand registered another five minutes. Cleo started grumbling. Then my father, still smiling, turned to the next teller at the counter and said for all to hear, "Excuse me, Miss. Could you let Miss P. Thomas know we're waiting on her?"

The teller turned, saw the young man sitting at a desk with the nameplate 'Miss P. Thomas' and began to laugh. The line behind us laughed. And the young man, embarrassed, returned to us smiling foolishly. Swiftly, he finished our transaction and almost saluted my father as he said, "Good day to you, sir!"

Thus began my secret respect, adoration even, of Daddy. I knew what I had seen that day was wisdom, and I wanted to inherit that, not the folly of the child neglector.

Now, two days after I had cut my hair, my father came for one of his visits. He looked at me sadly and said, "Jo, I take yuh out of Africa and yuh gone back?"

"What yuh mean?" I said.

"You had nice, long hair. Now you looking like a pure Negro."

Shocked, I could only stare at him. I knew my mother to be racist. She, who is as black as rich, French chocolate, always swore her days of girlhood on the beach were what had burnt her skin. My more Chinese-looking sisters teased me about my thick lips and nigger hair, but never did I expect my Chinese father to be racist.

Anger replaced shock as I shouted, "Yuh racial and yuh marry Mummy? And yuh living with a black woman now to boot?"

I stormed outside and went on the swing. When I saw my father coming I told him I did not want to hear his stupid apologies, I was not sorry for being rude.

Still he came, sat next to me, and said instead, "Jo, this is a racial world we living in. If you have something to use that could help you, use it. Doh make things harder than they done going to be."

Stunned by his honesty, I remained quiet, unsure what to say, what to feel.

"Listen," he continued, "it have a whole set of jobs you wouldn't get because you not a man. It have a next set you wouldn't get because you not white. Now you just add a whole next set you can't get because you black."

"I doh care about that!" I said hotly. "If I black, I black!"

"Yes. But that's just it. Yuh not black."

"Well, I not Chinee either!"

"Listen, just make sure you know what you in for. Once you know that and you still want to do it, go ahead."

As he got up and started walking away, the questions burning inside rushed out and I slammed them into his back.

"Why yuh marry her then?" I was crying now. "Why yuh didn't use what yuh had and marry a Chinee woman? Yuh know what you was in for?"

Sure he couldn't answer, I expected him to walk on, like he had done since the beginning. Instead he stopped, turned around, and I saw why humour lived in those eyes, for without it they were as still and empty as defeat, and he said, quietly, "Because … I didn't love nobody else."

For one moment, the weeds that stifled our relationship were uprooted and I saw a father and a friend. I knew I looked into the eyes he kept only for himself, the ones that knew he had chosen to laugh instead of cry for all the doubting and rebuking he did with himself, for the choices he had made and the ones he had not. Yet pain and puberty made me challenge those eyes.

"Well," I said, "like father like daughter, I choosing self no matter what."

He lifted his hands.

Pleading?

Giving?

But I rushed on, afraid to see, afraid to hear. "So I will do what I have to do, right? No matter how hard it make life."

I pushed my legs hard and let the swing carry me.

Away.

My first boyfriend – if our meetings on the Promenade could qualify him to be called that – was Paul Manson: tall, cute, dark, with Derek Leechung dimples! One of the 'soul boys', he wore his Presentation pants tight and gun-mouth (a style that would today surely classify him as gay, but back then it was the way the cool fellas made the statement that they were cool), with his shirt sleeves rolled up; and, of course, he had an Afro. Everything about him said 'hard man', and of course the Josephine Chin who had pursued Roger John relentlessly seemed to have a penchant for these men who had TROUBLE written on their foreheads. If I didn't know I had rank in Convent and among the boys' schools before, I knew it when Paul started checking me.

Long gone, though, were my days of unrequited love and shameless pursuit of Roger John. Now, somewhere, somehow, I had learnt the fact that I was the pursued and the boys were the pursuers; now I played the nonchalant flirt with total finesse.

I first met Paul on a Saturday. The event was Presentation's May Fair; I was in Form Two and only allowed to go because Cleo was going. Of course, she was going to meet her boyfriend, Allan, and she knew that I knew this, so she encouraged Mummy to let me go with her so her cover would not be blown. Anyway, Mummy's assumption that Cleo would keep an eye on me was dead wrong. Cleo lost me as soon as we walked in the gates of Presentation, and I breathed *good riddance*. My friends Jean and Carol were there as we'd arranged, and we wasted no time in checking out the games and the guys.

It didn't take me long to realize I'd inherited my grandfather's vice; he, the story goes, gambled away his second wife. I found myself by the Lucky Seven table, thrilled by every dollar I won back after the many I lost. And then, just when Carol and Jean had convinced me I'd spent enough money, a new attraction kept me at the table ... Paul Manson, coming on to take up his shift. Next thing I knew, I was getting first-hand advice and preferential treatment, and those sexy dimples kept me there another hour, somehow winning back money even when my bet was wrong, grinning with my conspirator, and in general having a ball. I only stopped when Jean and Carol threatened to leave me.

As I started to walk off, Paul grabbed my hand.

"Wait!" he said.

I turned round in surprise, pulled my hand away.

"For what?" I said.

"I …" he smiled (the dimples … the dimples!). Annoyed just a second before by his actions, now I was smiling.

"Well?" I said.

"Yuh done. Play? I mean …"

"Yes," I said, grinning, as he looked for his confidence somewhere between my face and the air behind me. "We going to get something to eat."

"Well … I mean … yuh could lime here instead." He nodded in the direction of a group of giggling girls standing not far from where I was, interspersing their laughter with bold looks at him and vengeful ones at me.

The old St Maria's posse – Caroline, Gillian, Wendy …

"No way!" I said. "I have to go. Bye."

"Well," he scratched his head. "Yuh … going to the Disco?"

"Sure," I said. Ha! Even Cinderella's curfew was late compared to mine. Six o'clock I had to be home by. Just when the Disco was starting. He grinned, relief flooding his face.

"Good!" he said. "I'll see yuh then."

"Okay. Bye." I started walking off again.

"By the way," he called. "I'm Paul."

"I'm Josephine," I called behind me without turning around.

"I know!" he called back.

I stopped, turned around fully, gaped at him. He grinned and shrugged his shoulders.

"Everybody know who Josephine Chin is," he said, shy again.

Carol pulled me. "Yuh feeling nice, eh?" she said as we walked off. "Josephine, yuh going to the Disco for true?"

"No," I said, "but I couldn't say that and sound like a nerd."

"But yuh make the boy feel he will see yuh there!" said Jean. I shrugged.

"And yuh know yuh like him, Josephine," she continued.

"Well, what yuh expect me to do?" I said.

"Well, how yuh will see him?" she demanded.

I shrugged again, this realization making me temporarily subdued.

But I shouldn't have worried, for there he was, waiting on the Promenade Monday evening. As my friends and I crossed over the road, Jean pinched me hard on the arm.

"Ow!" I yelled, pulling away my arm and glaring at her, "What yuh do that for?"

She grinned, nodding her head in the direction of the Promenade.

"Look," she said.

I turned to where she was looking. He was leaning against a tree, hands in his pockets, looking too flipping cool.

"Oh God!" I whispered, grabbing Carol's arm. "What to do?"

Now he was coming up to us. To me.

"Hello," he said, smiling at all three of us.

"Hello," I said, walking past him and up to Miss Judy's doubles cart.

"Why yuh do that?" Carol hissed at me under the safety of Miss Judy's umbrella.

"What?" I said.

"Why yuh didn't stop and talk to him?"

"I doh know. What to say?"

We snuck a peep at him. He looked as confused as I felt, standing where he'd met us, his hands back in his pockets.

"Go and talk to him," said Carol, pushing me.

"No," I snapped, pushing her back. "I wouldn't know what to say."

"Go nah, girl," said Jean, pushing me now too.

"Come with me," I said.

Miss Judy looked from one to the other, smiling, not bothering to ask what we wanted today. We turned and walked back to him, just as he started walking off. Once again, I found myself in front of him.

"Hello," said Carol.

"Hi," said Jean.

He cleared his throat, looked from one to the other of us.

"Ah ... hi. I'm Paul," he said, shaking my friends' hands, and then he was looking at their backs, as they pulled each other and walked off, leaving us there.

Eventually, we looked at each other and, somehow, started to talk.

And that was how my first romance started. Every day, Paul would come to the Promenade and I'd walk over with my friends, and they would continue walking up to Miss Judy's stall, while I would stand and talk to Paul. We talked about school and home and music and I don't remember what else. He told me he lived with his mother; his parents were separated. I didn't tell him I was the same. Sometimes, Carol and Jean would stand by Miss Judy, eating and macoing me, and I would catch grins from them. Sometimes I didn't notice them, only the poui flowers at my feet as I bent to hide the blushing that Paul's eyes and dimples and words brought.

After a couple of weeks, Gillian came up to me with, she said, a message from Caroline.

"Caroline say to leave she man alone," she said, standing arms akimbo in front of me on the corridor one day.

I looked at her calmly, seasoned from my days at St Maria's. Never before had I heard such language, yet I said, placing my hands on my hips, "Are you Caroline's messenger?"

"Doh worry 'bout that," Gillian snapped. "Just make sure and listen while yuh talking yuh show-off English! Caroline say to leave she man alone, yuh hear?"

"Well," I said, aware that my mother would have been scandalized to hear me, "tell Caroline to tell her man to leave me alone."

With outrage and something else, Gillian's eyebrows raised, her mouth dropped open. I turned around and walked off.

But I was angry. When I saw Paul later, I passed him straight. He caught Carol's eye. I saw him mouth to her, shrugging his shoulders, "What happen?"

Carol cut her eyes at him and grabbed my hand, pulling me to walk faster.

He finally caught me a couple of days later, stepping out in front of me from behind a tree, and I had to stop or bounce into him.

"Josephine," he said, holding my arm, "what happen? What I do?"

I glared at him, pulled my arm away.

"Let go my hand!" I said.

He let me go, said again, "What happen, Josephine? Why yuh not talking to me?"

"I didn't know yuh was Caroline man," I snapped, my eyes so angry that he stepped back.

"No," he said. "I mean, we used to go round, but we break up now."

"Well, yuh better tell her that."

"What she tell yuh Josephine?"

"How long yuh break up?" I asked.

"Since last holidays," he said.

My eyes pierced into him. "Yuh sure?"

He nodded. "Yes, Josephine. Yes. I sure."

I started to walk across to Miss Judy. He matched my angry strides. Of course, being more than a foot taller than I, it wasn't hard, but I wanted to make a point, and I think he saw it.

Just under Miss Judy's weary umbrella he said, reaching out to hold my hand, "Listen Josephine, I doh know what happen, but …"

"What?" I said, staring at him with eyes that blazed fire still.

"Caroline … well, Caroline is nothing. After *you*, Caroline is nothing. Nobody is."

I stared at him, something in my inexperienced, doubtful heart telling me that this moment could be a turning point in our relationship. But it was too much. I shrugged, smiled.

"Well …" I said, turning eagerly and gently pulling my arm away, glad for Miss Judy's enquiries about what I wanted, taking my time choosing doubles and chow and anchar I had no feeling to eat.

Gillian sauntered up to me the next day.

"Caroline want to fight you for she man, yuh know."

"She'll have to fight herself," I said, "because I not fighting for no man."

The surprised and something else look she'd had the other day, when I first answered her, came back again. She moved in closer to me, her voice dropped.

"Yuh know," she said conspiratorially, as if we were friends, "Paul break up with Caroline since last term. But that is the first fella she had sex with and like she gone crazy."

I stared at her.

Sex?

SEX?

Sex was a whispered word, not an action! Sex was a thought, not something real. Besides Cavelle and the white girls, I had thought we were all virgins. I had thought they were the odd ones out, not …

Gillian patted my arm.

"Yes, is true," she said, smiling, "they break up since last term. Doh worry with she."

The fact that Paul had spoken the truth played second fiddle to this new truth. This shock. SEX. Was it only me? Me and my friends, Carol and Jean?

I walked off from Gillian in a daze, questions pounding in my head. *What the hell did Paul want with me now then? Didn't he get what he wanted? Didn't my mother say all men wanted was sex? So why did he break up with her? And why was he going around with me? Was I to be his new conquest?*

All day my friends asked me what was wrong. I was not the usual laughing, talking Josephine. But I couldn't tell them. Carol and Jean knew about as much about sex as I did – nothing. With five older sisters, I could think of none I dared ask except Jessie, and she was quite up Arima. When I saw Paul later, he too asked me what was wrong. Worse yet, I watched him with suspicion – did he brag to his friends about him and Caroline? Were they waiting to see if he'd get through with me? Taking bets?

I remained in this confusion for I don't know how long. Though I continued to meet Paul, there was this huge secret between us, like a cloud that kept me from seeing him. Yet he rallied, filling my long silences with jokes about what his class had got up to that day, talking about the latest songs, and generally carrying on an enthusiastic one-man conversation.

After toting this load for weeks, I confided in Carol what Gillian had told me that day. The way her Chinese eyes turned into flat saucers stopped me from further discussion. I carried my questions and confusion, now more ignorant of men than I'd been before.

It was a few days before the end of term and Paul was getting on antsy. I finally found out the reason for this.

"So, what yuh doing for the holidays?" he asked one evening.

"My mom taking me and my sister to Barbados," I said.

"Nice!" he smiled, teasing me with those dimples. "Hope you doh meet any cute fellas there and forget me!"

"Who say you cute?" I flirted back.

He threw his head back and laughed. But when he looked at me again his eyes had changed, and though he smiled, his tone was serious.

"Listen, Josephine," he bent closer to me, "I could see you over the holidays?"

"Yuh crazy!" I snapped, jolted out of this slow, easy mood. "My mother will kill me!"

"Well … I mean … what if my mom called? You know … to ask her …"

I bent my head, shaking it violently.

"I mean," he continued, quickly now, putting out his hands to appease me, "I could ask her, you know … if she would, I mean, maybe you could come for dinner …"

But all I could do was shake my head, wanting him to stop. Needing him to stop.

"Josephine."

I looked up.

"I want you to meet my mother."

I was too naïve to read the look in his eyes. Too paranoid about men to understand the enormity of what he had said. Too afraid of my mother.

"No," I said. "No, Paul. I can't."

In later years, when I saw that look on a man's face, shut down and shattered by me, I would understand what happened that day.

"Okay," he said. "Okay."

We tried to continue talking, but it was all wrong.

On the last day of school, Paul had another proposal for me.

"Do you want to go up by school?"

"Which school?" I asked.

"Mine …"

"Why?"

"Well … you know … is last day …" He made circles in the dirt with the toe of his shoe.

"So?" I snapped, irritated.

"Well … yuh know, a lot of the fellas come up there with their girlfriends …"

"And?"

He looked up at me, a mixture of irritation and pleading, "Oh God, Josephine! I mean … I can't even get a lil kiss?"

"Oh."

We stared at each other, either tension or heat making us unable to look away.

I shrugged. "Okay," I said.

Paul's eyes opened wide. I started walking, realized he wasn't next to me.

"So now you not coming?" I said, turning around, grinning at him.

"You say 'okay'?"

I nodded.

"Yuh sure?"

I nodded.

He grinned.

I'm sure we didn't talk much on that walk. I wasn't nervous, but Paul was. He kept putting his hands in his pockets and taking them out. I don't remember much about getting there. But I remember this – walking to the benches at the side of the enormous Presentation College football field that I'd heard so much about from Paul. The sun we'd just walked through was now in front of us, mellowed because the field was nestled at the bottom of San Fernando Hill. I remember him sitting on the higher bench and me on the lower one, both of us looking at the sun, the mountain, the field. Me, suddenly shy. I remember him saying, "Come up here by me, nah."

And I remember sliding up, without looking at him, and him leaning towards me, so that I could only feel the sun now, as I closed my eyes, and his lips, soft and warm and full, were on mine. I remember the taste of dinner mints and a soft, gentle tongue and a light hand at my waist, and a light, light feeling in my head. And no amount of practising on the mirror had prepared me for this. This sweet innocence of my first kiss.

And when I opened my eyes, no longer shy, I remember that I was only more confused.

So we parted for the holidays and, I confess, despite that kiss, I thought little of Paul when I was in Barbados, flirting with boys and, in the Sundae Shoppe next to Accra Hotel, getting free ice-cream from a very cute beach-blond Rasta, who wanted to take me on his motorbike across the island; which, of course, my mother vetoed.

When we returned home, some new neighbours had moved into the house next door, and I soon became great friends with the girl, Kay, who was a year older than I. An added attraction was her eighteen-year-old brother. Paul was in another place and another time. But sometimes, when I looked in the mirror, I would touch my lips and remember that sweet Friday evening, and I would say to myself, *You have been kissed*.

And this would shock and excite me.

So when Gillian gleefully told me, on the first day of school, that Paul and Caroline had made up over the holidays, the first thing that was hurt was my ego, because by lunchtime, everyone knew, and Caroline and her crew kept passing me and smirking.

But in the evening, when I saw Paul on the Promenade and started automatically walking towards him, stopped only by Carol's and Jean's hands, pulling me instead to Miss Judy's umbrella, I felt I could cry then. And when I turned to go back to school and caught Caroline looking adoringly up at him, I felt I could have slapped them both. As my friends and I reached the school gate, a hand touched me from behind. I spun around to face Paul.

"Josephine," he said.

I pulled back from him, fire spewing from me.

"What?" I said.

"I sorry … is just that …"

"Is fine," I said, starting to walk off.

"Josephine, wait."

I turned around. He looked at Carol for help. She shrugged and looked away.

"Josephine, is just … you know, I couldn't see you … Caroline came over, it just …" he shrugged, "it just happen … yuh know?"

"That's fine!" I snapped. "At least you'll be getting some sex now!"

He stared at me with shame and surprise and something else. Regret, perhaps?

And ego reared.

"Besides," I said, grinning, "I had a great time in Barbados too!"

I did a perfect catwalk turn, and walked into the school gate, Carol and Jean and I howling with glee from the look of pain in Paul's eyes.

By the end of the second week, I heard from Paul's friend who was checking Carol that Paul kept talking about me in school. About how much he'd missed me and how foolish he'd been.

"Take it to someone who cares," I told Junior. I really didn't want to hear about Paul and his stupidness.

And then Caroline and her crew started cutting their eyes at me. Apparently, all was not well. Then Gillian grabbed my hand one day and shoved a note into it.

"What are you?" I snapped, pelting the note to the ground, "The flipping TT Post?"

"Oh, God! Why yuh so, girl?" she snapped back at me, bending to pick up the note. She held it out to me. "Here," she said.

"Who it from? Caroline?"

"No. No. Is Paul."

I steupsed. "Whose side you on anyway?" I asked.

She shrugged, looked embarrassed, but it didn't last. I started to walk off. Gillian pulled me from behind.

"Josephine, read it, nah! Oh, God, the fella really like yuh!"

I pulled away.

"Tell Paul to leave me alone!" I snapped. "He made his choice."

But if she did deliver this message, which she should have done well, he ignored it, coming to the Promenade every day, inducing his partners to mill around with him, watching me, waving and smiling and making a damn ass of himself.

One day, under the tired ears of Miss Judy's umbrella, Carol turned to me, shaking her head.

"Poor fella," she said.

I stared at her.

"You too?" I said

"God, Josephine. You not sorry for him?"

"No," I said.

She smiled wickedly. "Check him, nah. Trying to look cool."

I turned; saw him looking at us out of the corner of his eyes, those tell-tale hands flirting with his pockets.

"It good," I said.

"Josephine, stop punishing the boy, nah."

I steupsed.

"You know he like you," she continued.

"Shut up!" I snapped.

Then she was smiling and nodding and looking behind me. I turned around, and there he was, in front me. I turned back to Carol, who was walking off quickly.

"Nice!" I shouted at her back, "Very nice, friend!"

"Josephine," Paul said, "you ever going to talk to me again?"

"For what?" I said, turning to him.

"Look, Josephine, I sorry. I was stupid."

I steupsed, folded my arms across my chest, stared into the space behind him, hoping I looked bored, but what I had thought I'd forgotten, I realized now I had not.

"Look, Josephine, seeing you again … make me remember … what you want me to do?"

I stared at him in suspicion, wondering how he'd read my mind.

"You want me to beg? I'll beg. Please, Josephine. One more time … please?"

"You just forget about me for the holidays and pick up with Caroline and expect me to be cool?"

"No. No, I doh expect that …"

"Well, what you want from me then?"

"To forgive me. Give me another chance. I was real stupid."

"What happen? Sex is not enough? You not getting no sex from me you know."

"God, Josephine! God!" He pressed his fingers to his forehead. "Is not that!"

"What then?" I demanded.

He stared at me incredulously. His hands slipped into his pockets. He shrugged.

74

"I just like you, Josephine. I like you. Plenty."

I stared back, doubtful, confused, my mother's constant mantra reverberating in my head, punctuated now with many, many question marks.

Eventually I made up with Paul. But it was different, for me anyway. Maybe it was the Caroline thing. Maybe it was that I knew how much he liked me and it got too corny, or too much. Maybe it was that I didn't trust him.

Maybe it was, that if I did, it would make my mother a liar.

And so, at the end of that term, I broke up with him. I just walked to the Promenade and handed him the poem he'd written me during his math test and the chain and his brown plaid kerchief that smelled of his cologne. And while he took them, his eyes opened wide and he kept saying, "Wha's this? What you doing, Josephine?"

"I sorry," I said, "this not working."

"What? Why? What I do?"

"Nothing. Is me, not you," I said.

He held the things back out to me. "God, Josephine! You doh want to talk about this?"

I shook my head hard, like the day he'd asked me to meet his mother.

"I doh want these things back," he said, shoving the things at me. "Is yours."

"No," I said, backing away.

"Look, Josephine, I doh want them back. I mean, is yours. This doh change that."

"No," I said again.

"Why?" he asked.

"Because," I looked at him, "I doh want nothing of yours."

He stepped back. Smiled. Bit the inside of his lip. I turned and walked back to the school gate, not knowing how cruel my words had been.

I never forgot that look in his eyes and, when I saw him years later and our eyes met, and I saw that same look come over them, it was only then I realized what I had done that day; how confused, inexperienced Josephine had, in one moment, changed a heart for life; or perhaps, less dramatically, bruised an ego …

After Paul there was a series of boyfriends, or rather, Promenade Conversers and Escorts To The Taxi Stand. Since boys were not allowed to call me, I gave no one my phone number, and my love-life was therefore relegated to trying to fit meaningful conversations into half-hour meetings in between my time with my friends and eating Miss Judy's doubles. I don't know if I was distracted or disinterested; my friends thought I was not over Paul, but it was not that. Poor Paul did not have a chance from the first time we broke up, even though I didn't know it then; I never really knew what it was, maybe I just didn't want a serious boyfriend.

Unknown to me, I got the reputation of being 'cool' and 'hard to get', and though the suitors came, they tested the waters with great trepidation. Besides being a great flirt, I gave them little room for wading in. While this seemed to make me a greater attraction, I myself couldn't pinpoint that unreachable thing inside me that flirted then backed off. I didn't know myself to be a tease; was it just that I wanted to have fun without getting serious? Or was it some question in me that I was afraid to have answered?

From Friday evening though, the old Josephine returned; the shameless Josephine who'd tormented poor Roger John's life for years now turned this undaunted, unreturned affection onto Kay's older brother, Dave. I'd go over by her to lime and coerce her into calling him. He would come, scowling and irritated by his little sister and her pesky friend, and I would gleefully enjoy his trite, two-sentence response to me. I wondered, with the dramatized pain of youth, if mine was the road of older men and unrequited love.

At school, Carol and Jean and I swooned over the latest love songs, meeting every lunchtime to sing Air Supply's 'All Out Of Love', in varying versions of lyrics and tune till we got it right, the lyrics at least. We'd wail at the end about being "all out of love and so lost without you", though neither of us knew who the "you" really was, for I certainly wasn't singing about Paul, and Carol was, at present, madly in love with Paul's best friend, Junior, and Jean was going steady with Michael.

By Form Three, somehow I'd developed this cool persona. Between this and my Afro and "mannersing Caroline" as Gillian put it, the girls who'd hated me in St Maria's tried to make friends now, at least some of them did, and my St Maria's days seemed now a lifetime ago. Not that I liked Convent, I hated it here too, but somehow, in Form Three, even the teachers who disliked me started to leave me alone. I developed this 'couldn't be bothered' attitude that escalated my social life and sent my academic achievement plummeting.

Later, when I became a teacher, I realized that what I saw then was, in large part, a weariness on my teachers' part. What they took for laziness and lack of trying on my part was, however, my lack of knowledge that I had intelligence to tap into. Even though my mother gave classes at home and I would sit in the corridor, flirting with cute Sean Ash, when her back was turned and giving him answers to work that was far more advanced than what I was presently doing at school, there was no understanding on my part that I was smart. My anti-school days from St Maria's had been so effective that I treated school, and consequently my school-work, with a bored disdain. With ease, I topped first place in subjects such as literature and history and language, and with the same ease came last in physics and chemistry and, of course, math. Spanish and French teachers, after getting over the initial shock that I did not have an aptitude for their subjects as my older sisters had, generally left me alone. Even younger teachers, who had wooed me in Forms One and Two, now, seeing me develop more interest in boys and badminton, regarded me with a resignation that seemed to suggest that if I could, with little effort, come first in their subjects, it was my lack of effort that made me fail the others. By the end of first term in Form Three, I had started a new trend that would take me through to the end of my life at Convent – placing in the bottom five of my class every end of term test. My mother ranted at first, but did little else, and my older sisters' analysis that I was lucky to be ignored by Mummy fuelled in me a notion that, perhaps, she didn't expect any better of me.

While I could lose myself during the day at school with my friends and, on the weekends, next door by Kay, the nights were awful. There was only Dame Criss Cross, alias Cleo, and me at home now. Bernie came home late at night when I was already asleep and left before I got up, because she now worked in Port of Spain. Mary and Angie were long gone – Angie married and Mary living in Port of Spain.

Sometimes it wasn't too bad, I would watch television with Mummy, but often, very often, there were these terrible quarrels between Mummy and Cleo that left me tired and angry and alone. And this behaviour began a phenomenon that would last for many years.

At first it started with me just lying in bed and talking aloud about my thoughts and feelings and anger and frustration. Then, one night, while talking, I started to cry, and I felt something break inside me, and my tears stopped being sad and became tears of relief, and I could feel someone listening. Not listening with answers or questions or excitement like Carol and Jean or Kay, just listening. I felt I could say anything, think anything, and it would not matter; this listener would not be shocked or angered or disappointed. For the first time in my life, I felt free and totally, totally, accepted – just Josephine – and that was fine.

And in the midst of my crying one night I began to laugh, gently at first, then with great gusto, as this inexplicable feeling of love washed over me and inside me and I found myself filled with some kind of joy and peace that just replaced, suddenly, my distress.

I forgot all about this the next morning, except there was a calm inside me, a lightness in my step, a joy about waking up, instead of a dread of mornings that I'd had since I was five. I did not relate this to the night before; I just took it, as youth does, as one of those things. But that night, as I talked, I became aware that this was the freest conversation I had ever had. With no words or thoughts, I said everything. And as I emptied, I refilled, what poured out had emotions and pains and interpretations, and what flowed back in had nothing and everything. And when I was done, I was asleep, in some kind of deep, powerful rest, in no time.

Night after night, for many years, these meetings continued, though later they changed in a shocking way, but I know now how I stood those years of loneliness. These meetings became like my own private cupboard where I crept in and was removed from it all, where nothing could touch me and the day and the pressure and the doubts and the fears just oozed out of me and, instead of leaving me flat, blew me up like a balloon with something that had no name or description, something so all-consuming it floated me above all the tiredness and anger and everything else.

He was everything a mother warns her daughter about: older, more experienced, from a lower class; and of course, at sixteen, this smell of danger made me want him even more. Maybe it was my age, maybe it was untapped anger; whatever it was, I was on a warpath with my mother. If she said 'X', I did 'Y'. I goaded her into anger and revelled in our clashes, and when this boy, this man, came into my life, I knew what my mother's reaction would be, and I didn't give a damn.

Hayden came into my life much the same way everything else had happened to me so far – by chance; by me letting things happen, leaving things to happen, as if I had no choice or control in the matter. Sure he was cute enough, and injected my sixteen-year-old hormones with the powerful scent of sex that has ruined many sixteen-year-olds' lives, and maybe I really didn't stand a chance, maybe I didn't know what really hit me, but I was also standing in the road, waiting to be hit.

Presentation May Fair. Again. We'd smiled and flirted a little, but I had forgotten all about him the next day, until The Messenger came up to me in school.

"Josephine," called Gillian as Carol and I were walking across for our daily dose of doubles.

I steupsed.

"What she want?" I said to Carol.

We turned around.

"What?" I said.

She came bounding up to me, holding her skirt tight against her legs in that way that we Convent girls knew made the boys pant.

"The man like yuh, girl," she said, sucking on hot anchar and loudly sucking in air to abate the pepper.

"Who?" I asked, truly confused.

She steupsed and rolled her eyes at Carol. "She like to buss style, eh?"

Suck on the anchar, suck in the air.

I was about to turn around and walk off, then, "Hayden, girl."

"Hayden?" I asked.

She steupsed again. "The fella from yesterday."

"Oh, so?"

"He … sssssss … want yuh phone number … ssss … to call yuh."

"No," I said, turning and walking off.

Gillian grabbed my hand. "Why yuh so, girl?"

I pulled away and grabbed Carol, walked towards Miss Judy.

"Arright!" Gillian yelled behind me. "536-0992! He say call him!"

"Yuh going to call him, Josephine?" Carol asked me as we waited for our doubles.

"I doh know," I said, shrugging.

"Huh."

"What?" I said.

"He's a big man, ent?"

"Yeah …"

"Yuh could handle that?"

"Handle what?"

"What big man does want?"

"Doh all men want that?" I said, echoing my mother's lifelong warning.

Carol shrugged. "I guess so."

"Anyway," I said. "I doh know if I calling him."

I didn't. At least, not that day.

Gillian kept bombarding me with, "Yuh call the man?" and "Call the man nah, girl!"

And then one day, as I opened my homework book, this piece of paper fell out. I bent and picked it up, recognized Gillian's spidery handwriting, and there was Hayden's number. Curiosity got the better of me. Mummy was outside, wetting her plants, Bernie was not at home yet, and Criss Cross was locked in her room. I tiptoed to the end of the corridor, picked up the phone and dialled, my index finger poised over the little white button at the top that could, if I pressed it, disconnect me if I chickened out. The phone rang once, twice, three times, my finger started moving down, then ...

"Hello?"

"Hello," I said, "can I speak to Hayden, please?"

I could feel tension crackle through the phone.

"Speaking," said the voice.

I could tell he sat up.

"Oh ... hi," I said, "this is Josephine."

"Thank God!" he said, with so much relief, I laughed out loud.

So there was that little chink through my armour, and with each conversation, I became more and more fascinated with his ability to open himself so easily and show his heart. Fascinated and confused, beguiled by his readiness to express himself – a quality I was slowly losing – and bewildered that he did not seem to be the cunning, manipulative being my mother painted all men to be.

And that's how it began – almost as if I was peeping through the keyhole of a forbidden room, and I found myself wanting to go inside, for what I saw did not look as dangerous and scary as I'd been led to believe.

Of course, with all her warnings, Mummy had forgotten to tell us that there's a difference between the bait and the net, that the waiting and hoping brings out the best in a man, that of course we'd be tempted and reeled in just enough to throw everything we'd heard behind us. And Hayden, experienced man that he was, seven years older than me in fact, knew well how to hang that hook in the water and wait. I'm not saying he didn't mean it, in fact, in the end, he loved me more than I did him, but mothers should know that, at sixteen, truthfulness is more powerful than threatening. With every warning of my mother, I swam closer and closer to that bait, curiosity and hormones pulling me like a current, upbringing and fear floating away from me, as I moved instead to a smiling face and a reaching hand, even though these had betrayed me before.

For I had now reached the age where hearing only what is bad, and seeing for myself something good, made my mother's words a betrayal. I sought answers anew, outside of her, rejecting not just some things, but everything, and that is always the beginning of danger. For innocence lost can never be reclaimed as innocence, only either as wisdom or folly.

So it began, and continued for a long time. With each telephone conversation I became more and more fascinated; here I was, discussing such harmless things as school and music and fashion and friends with someone who was supposed to be The Enemy, and this was no innocent first love thing like me and Paul, this man was twenty-two! How innocent could this be?

Had I understood the mating game, the dance of desire, I would have seen this for what it was: curiosity, attraction, friendship. Instead, our relationship sent the thought pulsing through me that I'd been tricked. My fighter's spirit kicked in, and I set about finding things out for myself – building, as I did so, more distaste for my mother, a distaste which eventually turned to hate and my subconscious decision to break all the rules and go against all my mother stood for.

After a few weeks of telephone conversations, Hayden kept asking if he could come over. Of course I'd never brought any boy home before, but a twenty-two-year-old man is not contented with chit-chat after school on the Promenade and calling that going steady. I held him off for a few more weeks, telling him I'd ask my mother, but the desire to meet, the fear of my mother's reaction, the pressure he put on me, all came together in one word – deceit. I began finding ways of meeting him, which boiled down to me telling lie after lie. I would leave home for choir practice and he would meet me on the street before the church, I'd jump into his car and we'd go off, driving and talking and listening to music. Or I would say I was going to the cinema with my friends, and I would meet Hayden there.

Going around with Hayden also had a great impact on my social life at school, a whole group of girls who'd previously thought me snobby now befriended me, including Gillian. At the top of this list was a girl called Paula. She quickly replaced Carol and Jean, who were in different classes from me now that we were in Form Four, and became my confidante and shit-talking pal. She was no innocent like Carol and Jean either; many a Monday morning would find Paula and the white girls in the class yawning and hung over. Paula had freedom! Freedom I envied. Going out on the weekends with her older sisters, boyfriends coming home since she was thirteen, going to night fetes, a treat not yet afforded me. So when Paula started inviting me home, I was ecstatic! Of course Mummy put up barriers at first, but during the August holiday she relented. And of course, I went to my first night fete with Paula, clad in the latest fashion compliments of her wardrobe, and of course I met Hayden there.

The next day he came over by Paula, since I was spending the weekend there, and for the first time we kissed, on the steps under her house. Strangely, I don't remember the details of this kiss as I do Paul's, but I remember that it bore none of the innocence Paul's had, there was an urgency inside it that made me tingle with curiosity. While Paul's kiss had made me peaceful and content, Hayden's rattled me with an anxious need for something else. Maybe it was my innocence, or maybe it was his experience, but from the first, I knew this kiss would lead me to trouble.

One day, by telling some other lie, I met Hayden at the

cinema. We were walking back home, holding hands and talking, stopping every so often to kiss, and who should drive by but Bernie. My heart dropped into my shoe. Bernie's car stopped just after passing me. I grabbed Hayden's hand.

"Oh, no!" I said.

"What?" he said.

"That's my sister."

His eyes opened wide, our steps faltered. We were under a streetlight, so they could see us as clearly as we could see them. I could see Anna, Bernie's friend, talking to my sister in the car. I held my breath. And then the car drove off. Even though I exhaled, it was with minute relief, for I knew I still had to go home.

Hayden left me by the corner as I'd instructed him, and by the time I reached my gate my palms were sweaty and my heart had changed from R and B to Hard Rock rhythm.

"Hello," said my mother as I came through the doorway.

Now my heart completely stopped.

"Hi," I mumbled.

I looked down, waiting for the blast. My mother laughed. Dazed, I looked up, only to realize she was watching television.

"What happen?" she asked. "You not going to change yuh clothes?"

I stared stupidly at her. She looked questioningly at me.

"How was the show?" she asked.

"Good," I muttered, fleeing down the corridor as fast as I could without looking suspicious.

I changed quietly, so as not to disturb my mother's mood. All I wanted was to slip into bed and pretend this night never happened. Except for the part where Hayden had pulled me in to him and kissed me ... and kissed me ... But I was puzzled. Bernie's car was in the driveway, so she was home. Hadn't she told Mummy? Was she waiting to lecture me? Bernie was good at lecturing. She was the strictest big sister I had. So what was up? I tiptoed down the corridor; Bernie's door was locked. And where was Criss Cross? Was it my guilt or did the house seem to be holding its breath for a massive, earth-shaking exhalation? I tiptoed back into my room as my mother, seeing me from the living room, called out, "Josephine, look *Family* on. You coming to watch it?"

"No, Mum, I going to bed," I called.

Shaking my head, I pulled the sheets back and slipped into bed, glad for the warmth and comfort which, somehow, put me to sleep.

Bernie

Every Christmas, Bernie made sure our tree was laden with presents, stretching her salary from working at the bank into a massive stocking that encompassed every single cousin, niece and pumpkin-vine family we had. Me and Cleo used to stand back from the tree and stare agog at the mountain of beautifully wrapped presents.

Weeks before Christmas, the excitement would begin as Bernie would come home later and later, toting large bags and shooing us out of her room. We would stand by the locked door listening to the crackle of paper, and grin, pushing each other to get a turn to peep through the keyhole, as Bernie called out, "Move from that door!"

We would scamper away just far enough not to annoy her, but close enough to hear when the bolt was released from the door, and then grin at her as she came out of the room pretending annoyance, saying, "What? What? Those not for you!"

And we'd look from her to the parcels, grinning, because we knew that somewhere, in her cupboard, in her drawer, under her bed, were the many, many parcels with our names on them. And all this culminated in The Hunt on Christmas morning, Bernie having made sure to do a good job of hiding our presents the night before.

After the semi-slavery Mummy put us through each Christmas – scrubbing pots, scraping varnish, polishing the floor, cleaning brass, oiling fig leaves for pastelles, and washing up endless wares as she made sorrel and punch-a-crème and black cake – Christmas Day came as the final reward, a giant sigh after breath restriction. Our home, clean and shiny, would overflow with presents and people as cousins and sisters and brother would descend upon us for the day, and, with great excitement, we would lead each one to the tree, helping them dig in, squealing with the delight that surely Bernie felt, watching them unwrap something beautiful.

These were the Christmases I knew until 1979, when Bernie bought her first car, and in one Christmas I grew too old for my own good.

Bernie had been talking about buying a car for some time now; on the one hand Mummy encouraged it, seeing herself free from torturous school mornings, but there was something else, too, something about the whole deal that made conversation between them less and less and usually end up in a quarrel.

As the evenings wore on, getting closer and closer to Christmas, and still Bernie was coming home packageless, Cleo and I became more puzzled and aware of a growing tension in our home. Every evening Bernie was looking more and more sullen, and when she did come with a giant bag and met our grins with a tired shake of her head, not bothering to lock the door to wrap these presents, we understood this was no joke. Our home felt like a pressure cooker about to explode.

For the first time our tree looked bare. There were still presents, but nothing like what we'd grown accustomed to. As the countdown to Christmas sped up and the wave around our tree did not swell, a tide of something else grew.

On Christmas Eve we sat around the living room, singing carols that at first grew louder and louder to compete with the noise coming from my mother in the kitchen. Mary and Angie led our choir, but as Mummy's noise grew ever louder our singing became more and more feeble and first Bernie, then Cleo, went into their rooms. Eventually, I was left alone on the couch.

And then Mummy came out of the kitchen and walked past me in the living room and went into the enclosed porch where we kept the tree. From where I sat I could see part of her back, and I saw it shake, slightly at first, then harder.

"Mum?" I said, getting up and walking toward her. "Mum?" I touched her back. It stiffened so quickly, I pulled my hand away.

"What happen, Mum?" I asked, seeing now, as I stood beside her, that she was crying.

She didn't answer, just kept staring at the tree, sobbing quietly as she covered her mouth with her hands.

"Mummy?" I said, frightened now. "What happen?"

She sobbed harder, shook her head, finally whispered, "Look at the tree!"

"What happen to it?" I asked, confused.

She gaped at me. "How yuh mean what happen to it?" Her voice rose so suddenly that I jumped.

Her hands slammed into her sides. "It empty!" she wailed. "Yuh doh see it empty?"

She turned to face me, her face so filled with anger I stepped back and fell into the chair behind me. As the house waited with my mother's words echoing through it, I became aware of another sound, a far-away sound of a bolt scraping from a door, of a floorboard creaking, of footsteps, and my stomach knotted and rebelled.

And Bernie stood there, her eyes red, her face contorted, and she opened her mouth and choked and coughed and stamped, trying to talk but only sputtering. I watched the scene before me as if it was in slow motion, shouting, "Stop! Stop!" But I was only shouting inside myself. Shouting and shaking and silent.

Mummy turned to Bernie and said, "Yuh crying now? Yuh crying now and yuh new car park up outside?"

And this voice of acid reproach cut into my heart and made it bleed, spilling blood, and refilling with bile. And then, as my other sisters came out, shouting and quarrelling and doing for Bernie what she could not do for herself, I turned and looked at the tree, hating every stupid, material thing about Christmas, and the present I got that year was a bitter resentment for my mother.

Sunday morning, Mummy woke us up for church. I dressed quickly and quietly, not daring to bring unnecessary attention to myself. Sitting next to Bernie I snuck glances at her but could read nothing. Turning to shake her hand for the sign of peace, I looked somewhere past her face into the space behind her. My dread was immense. Back home I sat down to a breakfast of home-made bread and eggs and bacon that Mummy had stayed back to prepare. Feeling only a great weight in my stomach, I reached for the bread, knowing my not eating would bring the attention I so dreaded. I was pouring tea when Bernie said, "Josephine, how come you doh bring any friends home?"

My hand shook, tea spilled on the tablecloth, I looked at Bernie in horror. She turned from me and looked at Mummy. "Eh, Mummy? Cleo always have friends here but I doh see any of Josephine's friends."

"That's because she have no decent friends," snapped Cleo.

I glared at her but let it pass, praying for Bernie to shut up.

"Nonsense!" said Bernie, cutting her eyes at Cleo.

"Is true!" taunted Cleo, "Caroline and Gillian …"

"Those are not my friends!" I hissed at her.

"Well, I never stop her from bringing her friends," said my mother, highly offended.

"Well, maybe she doh feel they could come," said Bernie, "Eh, Josephine? Is that what you think?"

I stared at Bernie, my eyes imploring her to stop. I had never known Bernie to be so relentless. Why was she doing this to me? Why didn't she just catch me in a corner and buff me?

"And boyfriends," continued Bernie, "how come we doh see no boyfriends coming home?"

I turned away. God! I never thought Bernie could be so cruel!

"What stupidness yuh putting in the chile head?" snapped my mother.

"What stupidness? Josephine is sixteen now. It must have somebody she like."

My heart rattled inside me, ready to desert its post.

"I doh see why she have to bring any boy home!" ranted my mother.

"Yuh rather she meet them in the road?" snapped Bernie.

I lifted my head and stared at my big sister. This Bernie was not the one I knew who rarely stood up to my mother and who, if she did, was usually reduced to tears. This was more of a Jessie move. I gazed at her, willing her to feel my gratefulness.

"Cleo had boyfriends coming home since she was fifteen," continued Bernie.

"Is true." This from – Cleo? I gaped.

I suddenly realized what was going on. The unspoken tactic. Sisters against One.

Mummy steupsed loudly.

"Listen," said Bernie, "is better we see and know who Josephine liming with than we doh know."

"What liming? Where Josephine does go? By Paula and the girl next door? And by Carol and Jean, and I know them."

"All I saying is if Josephine have a boyfriend, she should feel she could bring him home."

Mummy steupsed again. "What boyfriend? Yuh have a boyfriend, Josephine?"

"Well …"

"Plenty boys like her," said Cleo, (*Cleo!*) coming to my rescue. "Pres boys does come on the Promenade to see her …"

"So yuh meeting boys on the Promenade now?" shouted Mummy.

" I …"

"That's not what I say, Mummy! They is just come to try and talk to her …"

"What stupidness!" said my mother.

"Mummy, Josephine is sixteen now, you know. She big."

I didn't know where to look. With exaggerated movements and plenty noise Mummy got up and started to clear the table.

"Anyway, Josephine, I doh want you meeting no boys on the road. Bring yuh boyfriends home, you hear?"

Silence, as Mummy moved off the table, cutting her eyes at Bernie as she did so.

"Yuh hear, Josephine?"

I nodded in the tremendous silence that followed. Not daring to look anywhere.

So that's how it happened that Hayden eventually came home, about five or six months after we'd first started talking on the phone. And of course he charmed my mother like he had me. Even though she was never actually friendly towards him, and she slammed shut the glass louvres promptly at eight to let him know his curfew had come, she couldn't help but smile at his over-eagerness to please her.

My beloved swing, that had been my womb through so many doubts and hurts and pains, now became my trysting place, as Hayden and I snuck deep, heated kisses made all the more delicious with the knowledge that all my mother had to do was look out of the dining room window to catch us.

Perhaps sensing the danger I was in of losing my virginity, or perhaps jealous that my Sunday evenings were no longer spent watching television with her, my mother became even more antagonistic towards me. I had seen Cleo go through this with her; now, apparently, it was my turn. The quarrelling grew and grew. At every opportunity, Mummy taunted me about Hayden.

"No wonder you can't do good in school, is that worthless boy you with!"

And now, every night, my silent meetings became demands on God to get her out of my life.

Of course Mummy didn't know that Hayden was no boy, and her antagonism towards him only made me want him more – not him, per se, but the defiance of her that he represented. While he thought I was falling in love with him, and indeed perhaps I was to some extent, the real driving force was my mother; the less she liked him, the more I did. And, not to be underestimated, his age and experience fuelled my sixteen-year-old hormones like wood in fire. By now we'd moved on to heavier stuff, his hot mouth on my hard nipples, his expert fingers kneading them to stand up even more; my body screamed for more and more pleasure and my confused mind questioned if sex was really so evil. My Catholic innocence and mother's warnings were ground more and more into the dirt every time Hayden and I touched, and were replaced instead by what must surely have been the heat of Hell, but Lord! nobody had said it would feel so good.

As Mummy pushed and poked, I stepped back and back, further away from what I was taught and told, and closer and closer into Hayden. For not only did he fan some flame that wanted to burn inside me, he became, too, my confidant and advisor on how to deal with this mother of mine, the ever-present burden that I knelt every night and begged God to take out of my life.

Form Five was winding down; I was faced with major issues such as CXC exams, what to do after school, heat and sex literally panting down my back; all this charged with the constant anger and quarrelling between my mother and me. I knew better what I didn't want than what I did want. I did not want to do A levels, I did not want to stay in Trinidad. I did not want to be anybody's sister, daughter, girlfriend. I wanted to be anonymous and unattached, in a foreign world where the name 'Chin' would not define me, so that *I* could define 'me' – whoever that might be. Secretly, I subscribed to foreign colleges, I spent evenings poring over the glossy brochures they sent me, seeing myself joyfully walking the path of my own life. I told no one of this, not even Hayden, for though he may have been my first love, I had this curious ability to compartmentalize my life, and this vision did not belong to him or anybody else. Only me.

I had always been good at keeping secrets. Nobody in my family knew that I wrote poetry and short stories; I hadn't even told my best friend at the time, Kay, though she had shared many of her own secrets with me. Nobody, not even Hayden, knew that I was seriously considering having sex with him after exams. And now, as I checked the mailbox every day, my brochures and dreams were held tightly to my heart.

Home was truly like a tomb now and I had been left to fight my battles alone. With Cleo gone I was on my own; even though she and I had not been close, at least she'd been there. More than anything, what had surprised me was how it was the day Cleo left.

"Well, you have the whole room to yuhself now," said Cleo, closing the last grip on the bed.

"Yes," I mumbled, surprised that I wasn't feeling more joy at the thought.

"So," Cleo sat on the bed and looked at me, "I guess I'll see you on the weekend."

"Yes," I said, unable to stop looking at the dressing table that now, devoid of Cleo's endless bottles of make-up and nail polish and perfume, looked stunningly stark.

"Well," said Cleo, getting up, "I'll see yuh soon, Jo."

I stared at the floor, astounded by the absurdity of tears in my eyes. One by one I had seen my big sisters leave home; some had left when I was still a little girl. I'd felt sad, but not overwhelmingly so. Now, with Cleo of all people, I was feeling this tremendous loss; as I saw the void she was leaving in the room, I could feel the same thing inside me with an intensity that surprised me. Cleo's arms embraced me stiffly. I hugged her back, pulling in my breath hard, to stop the tears.

"Well, see yuh." Cleo pulled away and smiled at me, just as I bent my head to hide the fat tear that fell.

"Oh, Jo!" said Cleo. "Is not like I going away. UWI is right there."

"I know," I said, looking up, surprised to see that Cleo was crying too. "I know … is just …" I shrugged, unable to define what it was I felt.

"Yuh here alone now," Cleo said.

I nodded. This had something to do with it, but there was something else.

A horn blew outside. Cleo's boyfriend, come to take her up to St Augustine.

"Bye, Jo," said Cleo, giving me a quick squeeze. "I'll come this weekend, okay?"

I nodded as I wiped furiously at my eyes. She left, and I sank down onto the bed, the same bed that Cleo and I had shoved and pushed each other away in, which now seemed absurdly big and empty. I rolled onto my side and faced the wardrobe, now made up of three messy shelves with clothes spilling out, and three empty ones. Now I had all the room I needed, could make all the mess I wanted without being nagged by the neat freak, and as my tears fell unchecked onto the pillow I finally realized what was crying inside, as my own voice echoed over and over the same phrase – *what a waste, what a waste*.

I hated home even more now. When I was home, I longed for school, which had become, ironically, rather pleasant, since my popularity among the rebels had grown with my Afro and going around with Hayden, and my teachers, weary, now left me alone to fail in peace; between doubles and good ol' talk, school was the best place these days. Sometimes, when I was in school, I thought of a hand or a mouth that had touched me somewhere, and then I longed for Hayden. And when I was with Hayden, I enjoyed with increasing rebel relish, partaking of the forbidden. And when, sometimes, I pictured myself in one of those anonymous American universities, and Hayden thought it was he who had drawn this sigh of deep pleasure from me, I would smile dreamily and leave him in his ignorance. Between my secrets and pleasures, I was enduring life, paying attention to everything I should not have been, and ignoring everything I should have been paying attention to.

Another development in my life at this time was that my father had started visiting regularly. Since he even came sometimes during the week I would find myself, for the first time, having him all to myself. He would ask about school and boyfriends and I would want to tell him, feel like I could tell him, and then stop myself, years of being unable to accept him as my confidant making it now difficult for me to open up. And whatever camaraderie I felt with my father would quickly be replaced by guilt and fear as my mother's voice, full of pain and betrayal, called me away. Yet despite this and the fact that, of all his children, I knew him least, I found myself gravitating towards my father. His soft voice and easy-going nature were like a balm in the midst of my turbulent life.

As if making up for lost time, my father started giving advice, not in a lecturing manner, but in a practical manner that made me listen, that made me think we were just talking, and only later, when he was gone and I replayed things in my mind, did I realize he'd been advising me. It seemed he came every weekend, and as Cleo came from UWI then too, he'd take us out somewhere: the movies, down High Street to shop, down Tesoro to show us off where he worked, to Beach Camp. For the first time I got my own glimpse of what it would have been like to grow up with him, and I liked it.

I remember a time he took Criss Cross and me to a lime at Crest Camp. We hadn't reached ten minutes before the boys started coming around, offering drinks, asking me to dance. But what I remember most is the look of surprise on my father's face, as if he was seeing me for the first time. Not fully aware of my own effect on the boys, I took these attentions in stride, finding it, in truth, more funny than flattering, that they would brave the father watching over me, like a protective mother hen, to come up and talk to me. And as any boy came up to me, my father stepped closer. At first I didn't notice, for he did it so well, but after about the fourth or fifth boy walked off, I began to take notice. A boy would come up, Daddy would step up, and then, somehow, begin talking to him. By the time he was finished asking the poor fella about school and parents and where he lived, the boy couldn't get away from me fast enough.

Briefly I wondered how Hayden would have fared, but though he'd been begging to meet my father I had no intention of letting them set eyes on each other, so I would never find out. Anyway, forget Hayden, I was getting annoyed with my father and Criss

Cross's stupid sneers. Then the absolutely cutest boy there came up, the one I'd been sneaking peeps at all evening, and I threw a cut-eye at my father, warning him to back off, and I stepped up so Daddy'd have no room for his little tactic. But my warning look and conversational abilities proved no match for my father's wiles. Cute Boy, too, succumbed to the same fate, and sadly I watched his back as he walked off. I spun around to face my father.

"Daddy! Why yuh doing that?" I hissed.

"What?" he smiled at me.

"Yuh know what!" I snapped.

"It good!" said Criss Cross. "Yuh too damn hot!"

"You just jealous!" I snapped at her, and turned back to my father. "Yuh running every boy that come to talk to me!"

"Not everyone," said my father, still smiling as he reached towards me and pulled my arms off my hips and held them in his.

"Yes! Yes, everyone! They all gone!"

"That's true," he said.

Exasperated by his indifference, I pulled my hands away and turned my back to him, steupsing.

"Josephine," he said behind me.

"What?" I snapped, not turning around.

"You must look for the ones that have staying power."

I turned around and gaped at him. As if he read my mind, he said quickly, "No, not like me. In the end, that's all that matters."

I shook my head, confused. My father always managed to throw me a catch when I was waiting to bat. Now, having dropped this great wisdom at my feet, he looked around the place with great curiosity, as if seeing it for the first time, and started discussing the facilities and maintenance with Cleo. I stood there feeling foolish, wanting to hug him and choke him at the same time. Eventually, to save face, I turned my back and ignored them both and started to dance as if my life depended on it.

Some time later, what was surely The Last of the Mohicans came up to me. I decided not to give my father the satisfaction of getting annoyed, so I mumbled my name to the outstretched hand and stood back, giving my father room to step up. And of course he did, throwing me a hearty smile as he started interrogating my new suitor with his offhand charm, pretending to put him at ease while all he was really doing was getting rid of him. Of course I couldn't get a word in, and when Barry turned towards me I expected the apologetic parting line.

Instead he said, "Can I get you a drink?"

"Yeah, sure," I said. Then, now hearing him, I looked up at him and said, "What?"

"A drink," he said, smiling, "would you like a drink? Coke, or something?"

I shook my head, too stunned to speak. Barry turned to Cleo and Daddy. "Sir? Miss? Can I get you anything?"

"No, no," said my father, smiling at Barry while conscientiously ignoring me, "we're fine."

"Well, then, Josephine, would you like to dance?"

Dumbly I nodded, casting my father a look. I don't know what was on my face, but his said, *Yuh see?*

If Hayden hadn't consumed so much of me I might have had time to like Barry. We talked on the phone and I found myself enjoying time with him more than I did with Hayden, but he scared me. "Staying power", as my father had called it, scared me, for I knew it would require of me something more than I could give. So eventually I stopped taking Barry's calls and started snubbing him on the Promenade when he came looking for me. Instead, I focused on Hayden, finding predictable danger less dangerous than stability.

Had we known what our father knew, we would have paid more heed to the regularity of his visits, but after a month or so of his coming almost every day, the sight of his orange bug at our gate no longer filled us with surprise. When he came during the week, I would find myself buoyed by seeing him, and when my father was there on the weekends, I staved off Hayden with excuses.

Right after Mock Exams – in which I did surprisingly well, coming third overall and first in five subjects, having secretly decided to reject my teachers' and mother's opinion of my abilities and test them for myself – my father started saying the weirdest things when he came over to visit. Once he told my mother to come and sit down to talk about his will. Other times, when tickling us or relating one of his colourful stories or corny jokes, he would suddenly stop and become quiet, he would get this incredibly sad look on his face that no amount of coaxing or teasing on our part could remove. Before our eyes, our father would turn from this wicked, jocular being into an old and tired man.

This was in March. Three months later, Daddy went into hospital for what was supposed to be a routine operation. He was supposed to be out by the end of the week. Then one week turned into two. We went to visit every evening after school. My mother never came but sent us with food for him. He would sit up in bed, joking and laughing, assuring us that the only reason he was still there was because one of the nurses had a crush on him.

By the end of the second week, however, more conversation was required of us, as Daddy would become quiet and pensive for longer and longer. Bernie came down from Port of Spain and drove up to work every day so she could see our father in the evenings. Mary came too, and Angie and Cleo and Jessie, and my big brother Jed who I usually only saw at Christmas and birthdays, all came on the weekends. Home was once more full of fun and teasing and my mother was off my case.

By the third week we began to get truly worried. In whispers we commented on how old he looked, how he didn't have the laughter even for his own jokes any more. We demanded answers from the nursing home and got none, only that he was too weak for the operation and they had to wait, but it seemed he grew weaker and weaker there.

Even Hayden's sexual spell over me faded, as I had little time for him now, going to the nursing home and then wanting to spend time with my sisters at home. Many a time the weekend would come and I would not be there when he came. I brushed off his pleas to meet my father, preferring to keep those two parts of my life separate. Even though he sometimes picked me up after school and dropped me off at the nursing home, I felt no guilt for not bringing him to meet my father. In truth, these days Hayden irritated me more than anything else, but since I was seeing so little of him, I decided not to rock the boat.

Besides, having my older sisters at home made me need him less, I had Jessie to confide in, Bernie to nurture me and hug away my worry, Mary to tease and make me laugh, Angie to keep me calm, and Cleo, who often sat and just held my hand. My sisters were here, and I relaxed a little. Some breath held in was released; I didn't have to fend for myself any more.

One night Jessie brought up what we'd all been thinking but been afraid to say: what if Daddy died? Everything ended in a quarrel with Bernie and Mary crying, storming out of the room, Angie and Cleo shouting at Jessie and eventually leaving the room. Only I stayed there, sitting on the bed. Me and Jessie. I turned to face her, my eyes opened wide.

"You think he will, Jess?" I whispered. "You think Daddy will die?"

"Is possible," she said, facing me even as tears streamed down her face.

"God, Jess!" I said, beginning to cry too. "I never really knew him."

"Do it now, Jo," she said. "Do it now."

"How? Where to start? What to say?"

"I doh know. Just tell him, he will find a way."

The next day, my father pushed away the home-made soup Mummy had sent and said, "Tell Nora to come." Then he turned his back to us and never spoke for the rest of the visit.

My mother went the next day. They talked quietly in the room after Daddy asked us to give them a minute. This only scared me more. I had never known my mother to be like this with him.

They said they couldn't operate because his blood was too contaminated by years of cigarette smoking. It had been turned to an ugly rusty colour that we tried to ignore the first day we walked in and saw it filling the bag hanging beside him. Now when we held his hand, we did it gingerly, trying to ignore the tubes that seemed to take up all the space. Or was it that the hand was so much smaller? We rallied on, telling our own jokes and stories, trying to ignore the pain in his eyes, the regret, the fear. It was the wrong thing to do, for he wanted so much then to tell us some truths, he needed to be serious, if only for a little while, but we were scared of what we might be told, and so, being our father's daughters, we covered everything with a smile.

And then my first CXC exam came – Commerce, a subject I was good at. And all I could see when they put the paper on my desk was my father's sad, empty eyes, and I wrote my name and rubbed my eyes, but still I could not see the paper and I could not remember anything I had revised the night before. Instead, I remembered every conversation I'd ever had with my father, every joke and story he'd told and eventually, I put my head on my desk and cried.

That to me was the end. The end of innocence, trust, belief. The reality of life hit me and I could trust nothing and no one. I could not trust life. Everything was temporary. Whatever suspicions I had picked up over time now heightened, I became a disillusioned sixteen-year-old, expecting betrayal in life, awaiting it in fact, and the carelessness that had characterized most of my school life, affected my work and which I had successfully challenged during Mock Exams, now returned.

I followed through with the motions of exams because I had no choice, putting on my uniform and going to school every day, pretending that, like my friends, I had only one care in the world – PASSING EXAMS! – while beneath, inside, I was old, old. Far too old for my sixteen years and my school uniform. I could not talk to any of my sisters about this, for this was not only my problem, we were all fighting the same grief, the same fears. So, accustomed to being secretive, I climbed back into my box and pretended, so everyone would leave me alone. Exams seemed such a frivolous pursuit, a passing chore in the work that was life, something to make us lose track of what was really important. And every day, after every exam, I trudged up the long flight of steps that led to my father's room, more and more tired after each day. Yet, as I reached the top, just before I entered his room, I put on a smile and the brightness of youth. My sisters thought I was so mature, handling things so well, and I was so far removed from myself, I often thought the same, except when I looked into the mirror and saw some old sad eyes staring back at me, eyes that looked like my father's – surprised by this new notion of life.

I seemed to be on autopilot; some exams I sailed through – wrote in a daze, remembering nothing while in the room, and unable to discuss the paper after, for I could not remember what had been on it or what I had written; but most of the exams found me caught in some strange time flux where my father and I seemed to be the only people in the world.

And eventually there came a time when our visits were not enough to bring our father back to the fun-filled man he had been. Our jokes were stale even to our own ears, our eyes that met over his head were wide circles of disbelief that knew, but could not accept, the truth before us. More and more often there was now silence in the room. Daddy would wait up long enough to see us all arrive, give us a weak smile, and then he would fall into a deep, complete sleep. Sometimes we talked about our day or remembered anecdotes with our father, but eventually we succumbed to silence as the room was truly filled by the tubes in his arms and up his nose and the bag of dirty blood, dripping, dripping beside his bed. And these things printed themselves into our minds and stayed there long after we had left the room, perhaps, in fact, for the rest of our lives. The threat of death would not be whitewashed by clean sheets and pristine walls, we knew. Deep inside, we knew.

One evening when we were all there, the woman Daddy had been living with came in. She started to walk towards my mother. Mummy shook her head violently and put out her hands, warding off the woman. We looked on in horror. And then my father raised his head off the pillow, pleaded, "Nora … Nora …"

My mother shook her head harder and faster as her eyes filled with tears. The woman stepped back, looked from my father to mother to us. And then my mother sobbed, covered her mouth and ran from the room. Tentatively, the woman approached Daddy's bed, slowly she stretched her hand out to his forehead. With surprising speed, Daddy turned his head away, and her hand fell to the pillow. She spun around, meeting my eyes with a look of confusion and shame and surprise, and I quickly looked down. She mumbled something and patted me; unwittingly, I jumped. As she turned, six pairs of eyes dropped to the ground and watched her feet back out of the room. We were stunned. And then Bernie, always Bernie, left the room, crying, searching out my mother to take her home.

So many unspoken words that day. So much regret and choice and what-ifs and whys that filled the room with the confusion and complication that life can bring. Explanations and apologies, left unsaid, seemed to pulse with a sadness and pain that was as real as my father lying on the bed. We practically ran from the room when the bell announced the end of visiting time.

The next day, I was standing by my father's bed when his best friend came visiting. For all Daddy's racist jokes, his best friend was as black as pitch and re-christened "Asphalt" by my father. But all Asphalt could do when he came was stand at the foot of my father's bed and weep uncontrollably. Covering his face with his hands, he shook from head to toe, and the child inside me longed to join him even while she looked on in horror, for it was really then that I knew my father was never coming out of there.

And it was that day that my father chose to ask me to sing for him and when I opened my mouth the trembling inside threatened to scream out, so that all I could do was close my mouth and shake my head and refuse my father his last request of me.

Mary

"No, Mary! No!" pleaded Cleo and I.

I pulled frantically at Mary's legs while Cleo reached up and grabbed her arm.

"I sorry, girls, I must," said Mary, looking down sadly at us from the footstool she was standing on. She pulled away from Cleo and turned her back to us, faced the open window, the hard concrete porch below; she stretched her arms out.

"No!" Cleo and I screamed, lunging at her and grabbing harder as tears streamed down our faces.

"Girls," said Mary softly, "is too late. This world is too cruel and cold. I have to go. You must let me go."

"No! No!" we cried. "Please, Mary! No!"

I clung to her legs as Cleo pulled so hard on her jersey, it ripped.

Mary sighed, turned around, "Aright, aright," she said, looking down and smiling sadly, "but only because I love yuh."

We exhaled with relief.

"Come down, Mary," I begged, still holding her legs.

She took another look outside, sighed, then slowly squatted down until she was sitting on the stool. Cleo and I flung ourselves at her, sobbing loudly and hugging her hard.

This had been the scene on many Saturday mornings for a long time; so long in fact that Cleo and I had other plans this morning.

"This is it, girls," said Mary, having locked us into the room with her and pulled the footstool to the window.

Cleo, then I, walked up to Mary and hugged her solemnly.

"Well," said Cleo, "it was great being yuh sister."

Mary looked at Cleo suspiciously.

"Bye, Mary," I said. "I'll always love yuh."

I glanced at Cleo, who quickly looked away.

Mary looked from one to the other.

"So," she said eventually, "all yuh not going to stop me?"

"No," I said.

"Is your life," said Cleo. "We love yuh too much to stop yuh if that will make yuh happy."

Cleo looked at me as I pressed my lips together hard.

"Come, Jo," said Cleo, as she turned the key in the door.

"Wait!" shouted Mary.

We turned around.

"So all yuh just going to leave me?" she demanded, gaping at us.

We nodded solemnly.

"Fine!" snapped Mary. "Just fine!" She pushed past us and stormed out of the room. Cleo and I burst out laughing.

Now, sitting in the waiting room trying to distract ourselves before returning to Daddy's room, I grinned with Mary as we reminisced about this incident.

"You and Cleo mess me up good that day, eh, Jo," said Mary, her face crinkling into the wickedest grin.

"It was good for yuh! Stressing us out with yuh dramatics!"

Mary snorted and sat up, she squeezed my leg hard.

"But I was good, eh? I had you and Cleo frighten every time!"

"You was too wicked," I said, grinning.

A loud clatter in the corridor made us jump. We gaped at each other. Mary grabbed my hand. Eventually I pulled away and walked to the corridor. I sighed in relief.

"Is nothing," I said, coming back to sit down by Mary. "One of the nurses dropped a tray."

"Oh," said Mary, rocking back and forth with her arms wrapped around her. "Oh, good."

For a while we had talked ourselves out of the place we were in, talked ourselves into feeling everything was fine, that we weren't sitting here, scared. Now we fought to regain this mood.

"Anyway," said Mary, stopping her rocking and grabbing my hand with such force I jumped, "it was all practice, yuh know. All leading up to my stage debut." She squeezed my hand and grinned.

"Yes. And poor Cleo and me were yuh guinea pigs!"

"Oh, God! Oh, God!" Cleo's muffled screams came to us from our father's room.

Mary and I froze. Nurses appeared from every corner, running towards our father's room. Mary and I jumped up, clinging to each other's hands. I practically dragged Mary toward the room. We heard Cleo scream out just as we reached the doorway of Daddy's room and then a blanket of white blocked us out, as the nurses pushed us back and shut the door. All I had time to see was a small, frail hump on the bed, and the smell of baby powder assailed my nostrils, then I was in the corridor, crying and clinging to my sisters.

And so, it came. The day of my father's death, and I could never again accept the friendship he had offered. I have always wondered, since that day, how a man's life, whether dramatic, dynamic, disillusioned or distraught, could end so unceremoniously; a gasp, a breath, and a being so important – somebody's father, husband, lover, worker, boss – becomes a memory, a used-to-be. This is as upsetting to me as it is liberating. That the efforts and people and things and time we worked with and for are in the end all left behind. That the things that tied us become the things we set free. That we aren't as all-important as we think. That we relinquish everything that identified who we were.

The anonymity I yearned for, found in, of all places, death.

Yet we cannot deny that how much we leave behind is determined by how much we give when here. There seems to me a great paradox here: to be important without being conceited, to teach while being the student, and in the end, our nothingness itself is the power. Our everything and our nothing; one and the same.

My father's funeral is probably the saddest event of my life to this day. For while the tears I cried in the big, impersonal Promenade church were those of anger and sadness for the loss of my father, the ones I cried in the old, wooden Erin chapel were for myself, for the self that understood too well, too soon, the reality of loss. People came up to me, saw my swollen face and startled eyes, and patted me and said inane things like, "You'll be all right," and "Doh worry. Doh cry so much." And while some part of me knew they were only trying to help, another part hated the shallowness of their words, the hypocrisy of this world, the demands put on us by society, to act 'normal' even while we are dying inside. In truth, I wanted everyone there to shut up and leave me alone, to say nothing, for there is nothing to be said.. With every word said to me, I shrank further and further inside myself, and with each false smile I had to put on, each assurance that I was 'coping', anger and resentment grew inside of me; death, men, my mother, all these became even more potent enemies, and the real enemy, fear, grew quietly, well hidden by the bravado of youth, waiting to pounce when I least expected it.

Now I no longer prayed for my mother to die, I demanded it. She had cheated me out of my father's love, she had lied about him and men in general being evil, she had denied me the chance to love my father and I hated her. Every night I demanded from God that he take her out of my life, and when He did not, I grew angry with Him too. Gradually, I shifted my trust off Him and onto myself; self-reliance became my faith and my motto. But I hid these changes well; my friends saw a quieter, sadder Josephine, my sisters saw a more mature one, my mother saw a more rebellious and hateful one, and Hayden saw a couldn't-give-a-damn one. I played roles to suit the occasion and no one, not even I myself, saw the real Josephine. I did not even know where to find her.

Though I still went to church every weekend and sang in the choir, these activities became just something to do. I had no belief in the church teachings any more; I shrugged them off as I did everything in my life. I stopped thinking things through and trying to make sense of them, for indeed, nothing made sense any more. Everything and everyone was a betrayal; if my own mother could lie to me, if my own father could die on me, what was there to trust?

Now that exams were over and everyone excitedly awaited results and talked about what they were planning to do next – everyone, that is, except me – a boredom and restlessness grew inside me; school and my friends seemed a world away from me. I shrugged away their questions and concerns, I shrugged away discussions on facing the big Life, and one day after school I shrugged away my virginity on Hayden's bed.

There was no fanfare. We were just fooling around as we'd been doing for a long time and then, as had been happening recently, he stopped and exhaled, lay on his back, ground his teeth and said, "Why yuh doh trust me?"

"What you mean?" I said, "I do trust you."

"Well, why you doh want to have sex with me?"

"Okay," I said, shrugging.

He stared at me, dumbfounded. "What?"

"Yuh want to have sex? Let's have sex," I said.

"Just so?"

I nodded.

"Yuh sure?"

I nodded.

If I had to choose someone to break me into the groove, I couldn't have chosen better. I didn't know it then but now I can say Hayden was a pretty good lover. He was just gentle enough, just urgent enough, and very loving. Yet I felt nothing, neither elation nor shame, the vacuum inside me was still there and because of this, because I felt no pressure to 'be' or 'do', because for the time it lasted I didn't have to give a damn about anything else, I loved sex. Here was abandon; here was the anonymity that I craved. Besides the physical release, sex gave me an outlet for forgetting. Sex to me spelled Freedom!

While quarrels between my mother and me had eased a little after Daddy's death, I could see her gearing up now, getting ready to pounce. Counting down the days for CXC results and getting back her strength in case she needed it.

And she needed it.

I failed five exams and passed four, not enough to give me a CXC certificate. Now there was noise day and night at home. Mummy egged me into face-offs and I did not back down, finding a wonderful release in shouting back at her. She ranted about my preoccupation with men as the reason for my failure, and confirmed what almost every teacher had said since I was five, I was duncy. She pounded it into my head that I was a disgrace, more so since my two older sisters were doing so well at UWI. And while I learned to fight back, part of me cringed in pain, words sank into me and settled themselves into the foundation of my being; to fend them off, I screwed and partied hard. Sex was power to me, and I found I could enjoy it with little connection, find, in fact, some detachment through it. It reinforced my truth that self-fulfilment and selfishness are the only survival tools necessary.

Yet while my mother tortured me for my lack of performance in school, she told everyone else that I had done so badly because my father's death had affected me. Perhaps she was making excuses for me to save face. If only she had talked to me, she would have known how true what she said was. Behind my back, she sought advice on what to do with this 'problem' and made decisions and arrangements for my life. She came to me one evening, demanding that I repeat Spanish and math at evening classes so she could get me back in school to do A Levels the following year. I ranted. I did not want to do this. She ranted back, did I want to stay and party whole night and do God knows what else?

Yes! Yes, I did.

Well, not in her house.

We went back and forth for weeks with this. And always, my mother got the last word, and always, I ended up crying.

One night it was especially bad. Crying, I opened the gallery gate and ran downstairs. My father's bug, parked in the garage since his death, seemed to call me. I opened the door and crawled in, hugging the steering wheel and sobbing. I cried as though I would never stop, I did not know I still had so many tears inside me. And when my tears started to subside and my sobs turned to intermittent hiccups, I became aware of a gentle voice, somewhere inside me.

"Jo, you want to be happy or not?"

"I do!" I whispered aloud. "I want to be happy, Dad."

"Well then, you have to make yuhself happy."

I lifted my head, looking for him. His voice was as real to me as the car I sat in.

"How?" I said. "How? Living with her?"

An image of my father shaking his head came before me, he closed his eyes and then opened them, watching me with that patient look he used to wear.

"She doh matter, this is about *you*."

"How?" I said, crying again. "How she doh matter?"

"Happiness is inside you," said Daddy, "is a choice."

"Tell me what to do."

There was no answer.

"Dad?" I called. "Dad! Please! What to do?"

Nothing. I waited. Closed my eyes. Still nothing. Only a tangible quiet in the car and, I suddenly realized, inside me. All the tears and turmoil and trauma, now far away, gone, as if a hand had wiped them away. I sat up. Wiped the windshield, looked out.

"Happiness is inside me," I said to myself. "Happiness is a choice."

I opened the door and got out. I still did not know what this meant or what to do with it, but I felt like I'd been given a key to some door inside me.

Without consciously meaning to, I stopped fighting my mother about my future. I settled into her plans for my life, enrolled in evening classes, and forgot about what I wanted. Maybe subconsciously I related happiness to peace, and peace meant putting a blanket on this spirit of mine. Didn't it?

Perhaps the only person who saw what was going on with me was Hayden. Though I said I loved him and greatly enjoyed our romps, he knew there was a part of me he was not touching. Sometimes he would look at me strangely, as if trying to bore a hole and see deep inside me, and he would say, "Josephine. Talk to me. What happen?"

And I would laugh and shrug and tell him he was being paranoid. Other times he would become desperate and angry, accusing me of shutting him out. Those times I would shrug and ignore him, leaving him pouting till he came back, apologizing. The truth was, I was not hiding or holding back anything from him, he just could not get in; there was a part of me that he could not see, because I had started collecting so many little boxes of me in the attic of myself that even I forgot their labels and contents.

The next year passed in a blur. I barely passed math and failed Spanish again, but at least I had my certificate. At least this would get my mother off my back. She began her quest of getting me back in school. I paid little attention; instead I partied and pretended. I lived carelessly, acting out my life on impulse, like an automated robot, going through the motions by giving the appropriate reactions to situations while in truth I was barely conscious. I was on the edge and so close to ruining my life, and no one saw it, least of all me.

One time I went to a birthday party and stuck the cake with the birthday boy. Somehow Hayden found out about it. He asked about the party, waiting for me to tell him, and when I didn't, he informed me that he knew I'd stuck the cake with this guy called Mark.

"So?" I said, shrugging.

He stared at me. "So yuh wasn't going to tell me?" he asked.

"No," I said.

"Why?"

"Is not yuh business."

He looked like I'd winded him.

"I thought," he said after a while, "I thought we were going around … I …"

"So?" I demanded. "That mean yuh own me?"

"Own yuh? No! I just thought if we were going to share body parts we would let each other know!"

I had never seen him so angry, but I couldn't have cared less. I steupsed.

"Listen, break up with me if yuh want, right. I not going to listen to this shit," I snapped, walking off.

He grabbed my hand, stared at me as if now seeing me. He pulled me to him. Exhaled over my head.

"Josephine … I …" he sighed. "Okay, okay, you win, right. Forget it."

"Fine," I mumbled.

What should have scared me was that I really didn't care if he'd broken up with me then or not. Why was I screwing with this man if I couldn't care if he was in my life or not? Was sex so meaningless to me? Were my body and heart so fickle? Was I really sharing myself, or was I just using him to fill some purely physical need? I didn't know and didn't care. None of these questions came to me then. I was just on my own beat, moving too fast to ask myself anything, far less answer anybody else's questions. All I knew was that I just had to keep moving. Stopping was the problem.

Of course what Hayden failed to tell me then, when he was so hurt, was that he'd been sharing body parts too, and it wasn't just his tongue, though I'm sure that came into play. Some months later, claiming he was feeling guilty, he told me he and his ex were still seeing each other off and on. While a couple months before I could have justified this by thinking he just needed her for sex, I couldn't dismiss it like this now. From his perspective, he was just a dumb ass, relentlessly pursued by his ex, who'd given in to ego and temptation.

"Just a helpless prick, then?" I asked, smiling.

He'd looked down, actually embarrassed.

On the surface I was angry, on the inside I was bewildered. So Mummy was right then? Men really were dogs? Maybe sex with one woman wasn't enough, maybe I didn't pursue him enough, make him feel wanted enough, or man enough. Or was it that, no matter what I did, this was bound to happen, just the nature of the beast? I don't know, but something in me died that day. Like Paul, it was just a matter of time for Hayden.

By the time I entered A Levels in Couva Convent, Hayden had started feeling like an irritating pet to me. I hinted at my need for space and all he did was get angry. I would purposely be out on the weekends when I knew he was coming, and school evenings I pleaded endless homework to escape him. More and more often, our telephone conversations ended in quarrels.

School now was a different experience; I was somewhat anonymous at this convent. Even though some there knew the Chin name, I was the first in my family to be here; there was no big-sister record to plague or compare me with. Whatever Chin impression would be left behind after I had graduated was up to me. I revelled in this. I was enthralled by this control over my life that I felt for the first time, and the best in me came out.

Before long, the collective agreement among my teachers was that I was smart. That outspoken spirit in me that had been called to order since I first set foot in school, was now wooed and celebrated. I found myself holding debates in class with my teachers, my essays were read out for all to take pointers from, teachers called on me when no one could answer, and I sorted through the rubble of insults and neglect and found, like once dusty jewels just washed and put into the sun, a confidence, intelligence and excitement about learning that I had forgotten when I put my curious little five-year-old spirit away.

This too was the year I stopped praying for my mother to die, for Hayden's revelation had proved her right, men were really dogs. Later in the year, his ex became pregnant for him; still I did not break up with him, finding it easier to avoid confrontation and simply ease away from him. Because of my ability to compartmentalize my life, I was not consumed all day long by Hayden and what was going on; while I was at school or with my friends, there was in fact no Hayden. And he, without knowing, had probably saved me from myself, had certainly saved me from that bitter hatred for my mother as disillusion brought light and I opened my eyes enough to see her.

Mummy

"Forty-eight!" said Bernie. "So much! How yuh get so much, Mummy?"

Mummy stared hard at the Scrabble board. "Check it," she said, shrugging.

"Is a triple word score, Bernie," I said.

115

"But still," said Bernie, "something looking funny."

"The 'H' on a double letter," I said, pointing to the board, "so that is eight, nine, the 'P' is three points and 'Y', no points for the blank – sixteen. Sixteen threes is forty-eight."

"Aright," said Bernie, still frowning as her eyes searched the rest of the board, looking for something. "Aright," she said again, and wrote down the score.

"That put you in the lead, Mum," I said, glancing at Mummy.

Mummy nodded, her eyes open wide as she pressed her hand to her mouth.

I turned the board to face me, "My turn," I said.

A strange sound came from my mother, something like a sneeze. I looked up at her. Her shoulders were shaking ever so slightly. I looked at Bernie, who was watching Mummy too.

"What going on?" I asked.

Bernie shrugged. Mummy shook her head hard, even as her shoulders shook harder.

"Wha's the joke, Mummy?" asked Bernie.

Tears were streaming down Mummy's face now, and as she moved her hand from in front of her mouth a loud half-gasp, half-scream, escaped. She slapped her hand hard on the table, making some of the letters jump off the board and finally she erupted into full laughter, pointing at the 'blank' she had just played, now turned over to reveal that it was, in fact, an 'A'.

"Mummy!" shouted Bernie, "Yuh cheat!"

"Ay!" I said, "How yuh could cheat boldface so, Mummy?"

Bernie and I looked at each other in surprise as Mummy jumped up from the table and, howling with laughter, galloped towards the toilet.

"Well, yes!" said Bernie, grinning.

I snorted.

We could hear Mummy still shrieking in the bathroom.

That August my mother took Criss Cross and me to Barbados for holiday again. This would be our last holiday together, since Criss Cross was now engaged. Having crossed a hurdle in our relationship she had not even known existed, I stole glances at my mother when she didn't know, feeling guilty one minute for the hatred I'd felt for her, and relief the next that God had ignored my stupid prayer, and mostly, mostly I felt humbled that I still had so much to learn. Now, as if seeing her for the first time, I noticed the smiles that crossed my mother's face when strangers on the beach asked her about Trinidad. When Cleo and I waved as she clapped us to come in from the deep, pretending we took her calling as greeting instead of warning, and she scolded us when we came out of the water, always telling the same story about when she and her cousin nearly drowned as girls on Erin beach, I listened with new interest, seeing my mother as a girl in my mind's eye and smiling at the wonder of it. When we sat for dinner and teased my mother about the elderly gentleman at table five who seemed to be always looking our way, and she steupsed and told us to stop talking nonsense, I could see despite her seeming annoyance, a grudging amusement at our irreverence.

Maybe it was me growing up, maybe it was that my mother flourished in anonymity as I did, but that holiday I could see a different something peeping out, and part of me sensed that inside her there was another person who she would have been, if only she had known how.

When I returned, I was told by Hayden that "she" had had "it". "It" turned out to be a boy. My boyfriend had a son. With another woman. I pondered this. I stirred it over and over in my mind. Still it remained like the lumpy porridge we used to have to drink every morning.

As detachedly as I'd done everything in my life so far, I broke up with Hayden. Just like that, one day at his house, I broke up with him, telling him I needed space. He refused to hear, throwing temper tantrums, pacifying, reasoning, everything, he tried it all. Like someone looking through the window at a scene being enacted, I saw myself playing the contrite girlfriend, even while I knew I just wanted to flee the room. He turned away from me eventually, and I found myself moving towards him, out of some strange sense of pity. But when he turned around and looked up at me accusingly, drowning me in guilt, some warning bell rang inside me, some memory of guilt carried without knowing why, and I stopped, stepped back, said words that had nothing to do with me now.

"I sorry," I said, but my tone and eyes said different.

He backed down, quickly changing accusation into hurt.

"I doh want to be friends," he said. "I never want to see yuh or hear from yuh again."

"Okay," I said, turning around and walking, walking, out of his room, out of his life, feeling only relief, relief that I managed to escape … what?

Now men and relationships were the furthest thing from my mind. Even sex was no longer a big deal. I was caught up in the euphoria of being popular at school. I was now school prefect and House Vice-captain, younger girls flocked to me to seek advice and settle disputes, teachers called upon me to sort out class issues and give motivational speeches to younger students; and though I loved all of this, I took it in stride, adding to my popularity by being 'cool'. And it was not a feigned coolness, but one that remembered so well its St Maria's days that it could never dream of being pompous.

So this was the kind of time I was having at school. Not only was I contented, I was actually happy in Sixth Form, my life needed no further excitement, so I was not prepared at all for the twist that Carnival of '84 was going to bring into my life.

Carnival is my favourite time of year, representing the abandon and anonymity I so often crave. Like sex, everyone is caught up in the moment; there is so much passion and energy that there can be nothing else. The same music you hear later in the year that sounds sometimes too loud or too fast then, is the same one that brings you to frenzy at Carnival time. Everyone taps in, whether at a creative level or at a party level; to something so big and all encompassing that it leaves us all breathless on Ash Wednesday. Collectively, the temperature rises at Carnival, and Trinidad pulses with a heat that sizzles with frenzy, the communal scream of stress released, as we jump and wave and wine for two days straight. So potent is this release that if you stretch your hand out you can feel the air thick and throbbing with life.

Carnival of 1984 goes down in the books as one of the best. The music that year pulsed with a sweet, sexual energy that made you feel to hold someone close even as you wanted to jump up in single abandon. Men like Baron, who had always been considered as ol'-time calypsonians by us young people, had us sweating and chanting about "Feelin' It!" even while he warned us that "Somebody Go Jam Yuh". Even old men like Sparrow, who hadn't had a hit song in years, had us screaming "Doh Back Back" while we back-backed into whatever hot, sweaty body was behind us, revelling in the tribute paid to sex and freedom at Carnival time.

That year Tracy, my friend from Arima, and I must have gone to all the best fetes, my big brother Jed willingly picking us up. I shrugged off Mummy's quarrelling and focused on what lay ahead. Tracy and I would spend hours choosing and exchanging clothes, often dressing alike. On this particular night we had changed clothes about ten times and were finally ready and impatiently waiting for Jed. Mummy's grumbles had quieted and we could hear her snoring in her bedroom, I prayed for Jed to hurry, since I did not want her to fall asleep fully so that we

119

would have to wake her up to tell her we were going; this would only cause more noise. We looked at the clock every five minutes. At twelve o'clock we grudgingly started to undress and then, BEEP-BEEP!!

He was here, finally!!

Jed

Just as I was wondering how I would survive my father's death and the loneliness at home, my brother, the eldest of us all, got transferred to South for five months and moved into our downstairs.

Of all my siblings, I knew Jed the least. Being twenty-five years older than I, he was long gone by the time I was eleven. Though he visited every August and Christmas with his wife and children he always seemed aloof to me, so much older, and I never thought of him in any other way than the distant big brother. Now, even though he was right downstairs and I was incredibly lonely, I was still tentative about venturing into his space.

Then one day he called me down to listen to some jazz, and we found we had this love of music in common. Next thing I knew, I was downstairs for hours, talking and listening to LP after LP until Mummy called me upstairs. Bit by bit, we started knowing each other. Sometimes, when he came home early, he'd take me for a drive and buy me a beer! Man, he was cooler than I thought!

And then one morning, bright and early, Mummy and I were at it. This had been going on for weeks, she nagging me about going back to school, me resisting. Now, though, she was wearing me down.

"I sure yuh didn't do good in exams," she began this morning. "Yuh should go now and see Sister Theresa and ask about repeating. Now, before the rush start."

I bit the inside of my cheek to keep from answering. She was not going to goad me into a quarrel this morning.

"Yuh hearing me, Josephine? Go now before school close. Go this morning."

"I doh want to repeat, Mum," I said through clenched teeth for the millionth time these last few weeks.

"So what yuh going to do then?" she demanded.

I remained silent.

Mummy came and stood in front me, arms akimbo.

"What yuh going to do, eh?" Her voice rose. "Yuh going to lime and party with that worthless boy till yuh get pregnant?"

I stared at her, fire burning in my eyes.

"Doh watch me so!" she shouted pointing in my face. "Yuh damn well going and ask to repeat, yuh hear? Yuh not going to shame me!"

I steupsed and pushed past her.

She grabbed my arm and spun me around.

"Who yuh walking off on?" Her hand lifted and slapped my face hard.

I put my hand to my face as my eyes smarted with pain.

"You!" I shouted. "You! I walking off on you!"

I pulled my arm away and stamped towards the back door.

My mother charged behind me.

"Come back here!" she screamed.

"Leave me alone!" I screamed back, as I reached the kitchen door and pushed it.

From behind she grabbed me. I spun around and pushed her, dodging the hand aimed at my face, I turned back to the door, and bounced into Jed.

He looked past me at Mummy

"Leave her alone," he said in a cold, hard voice, as he pulled me out of the door and pushed me behind him.

"Mind yuh business!" snapped my mother.

"This is my business," he said in that awful voice.

"Move!" Mummy shouted. "Move out the way!"

121

He moved closer to her.

"Doh move, Jed!" I shouted, pushing behind him.

"Josephine, go downstairs," he said in a voice I dared not disobey.

"Jed, I say MOVE!" I heard my mother say as I ran down the steps.

"I not going nowhere, Mummy. Leave her alone."

"What? Yuh playing big brother now?" I could sense my mother turning on him now. "Why you doh tell her how yuh nearly kill her aready?"

My heart stopped cold in my chest. I fled downstairs, not wanting to hear more. I walked to Jed's stereo and put on an LP.

Eventually he came back down, looking exhausted. I stared at him, not daring to ask. He sat on the couch opposite me and exhaled.

"Yes," he said finally. "Yes. I nearly kill yuh when you was a baby."

I waited. I think perhaps I was not even breathing.

"She and I was quarrelling," he said, looking at the wall now, as if he was seeing it all again, "and is the first time I get so vex. She hit me with a pot and I pick up a brick and fling it at her. And it miss yuh, lying in the crib. It miss yuh," he looked at me now, held out his arm, put his thumb and index about one inch apart, "by this much," he said, staring at me with the same astonishment I felt. He pressed his fingers into his eyes, exhaled.

"And I feel guilty for that ever since. My baby sister I nearly kill …"

I got up and sat next to him on the couch, put my arm around him.

"Well," I said, "yuh make up for it today."

The fete was crowded, the music pounding, and we couldn't stay vexed with Jed for long. We shoved our way through the clumps of people and elbowed some space at the bottom of the stairs where we could see and be seen. Tracy and I revelled in flirting; we used to get real kicks out of seeing how dotish the fellas would act. And with Jed here, we knew all we had to do was give him The Look and he'd come to our rescue. Since he was more than twice my age, everyone always thought he was our father, and this worked well for us – for Tracy and me, that is, I'm not sure how good it was for poor Jed.

Anyway, we were at the bottom of the steps, dancing and flirting and feeling our youth, when I felt Tracy's elbow jab me so hard in the side, I gasped.

"What the …" I snapped, spinning to face her, only to see her gaping up the steps.

I turned to look, and somehow my eyes had the sense to move in slow motion, for the vision before me could only be watched in all-acknowledging fullness, and I saw the tightest pair of jeans on the longest pair of legs – whose muscles somehow still flaunted themselves underneath the thick denim – and the flattest stomach and the broadest chest, with just enough muscular development to make a girl want to rub, not squeeze. And then there was this mouth looking like it was made just for kissing, and eyes that were shy and suggestive at the same time, pulling me in even as their owner looked surprised to be receiving all this attention.

He looked from Tracy to me and we, losing all finesse of flirting, instead stared shamelessly at this sexy red man coming down the steps, our eyes raping, stopping way too long on the bulge at the front of his pants. And suddenly he was in front us, looking from one to the other, saying "Hi!" in a tone that was curious and flattered and flirting and shy all at the same time. While we still had not regained consciousness and remained open-mouthed and staring, so that he moved on into the crowd behind us.

When we eventually turned to each other, we saw the astonishment in each other's eyes and said, at the same time, "Yuh stupid eh? Why yuh didn't talk to the man?"

And then we burst out laughing, sincerely grateful for the release it provided for the intense sexual instinct that had taken us both by surprise. Now, remembering our power, our control, we shrugged.

"Oh well," I said, "easy come, easy go."

We turned back to our task of monitoring the stairs while looking like we were not, and dancing and flirting. But somehow, after the passing of the red man, everything else seemed colourless. Eventually we turned to Jed and told him we wanted to go into the crowd. We didn't say it, but we were both thinking, God! I hope we see *him*!

Later, as the fete started to empty, we found ourselves suddenly next to him and his group of friends. And, as Carnival allows, we easily and smoothly ended up dancing together. Him and Tracy and me and his friend, who, of course, looked nothing like him. I was damned vexed but couldn't show Tracy, who grinned at me like the stupid cat that just ate the cream. And the thing we liked him even more for now was that he wasn't desperate and sweaty like the others, neither was he conceited; he was just cool. In fact, he was so cool that Tracy grabbed me at some point and yelled in my ear,

"I think he gay!"

I looked at her in shock, then behind her, up at him.

"Damn!" I shouted, glad for the too loud music, "What a waste!"

She steupsed, nodded and backed into him some more, flinging waist that had him looking down in surprise. I threw back my head and laughed at the "We'll see" expression on her face, and he, poor fella, unaware that his very masculinity was being tested, grinned at me too.

Next thing, Jed was tapping me on the shoulder.

"Time to go," he said, giving an amused glance at the group of fellas around us. He looked at Tracy and lifted his eyebrows.

"She dancing or fighting?"

We looked at Tracy and laughed; she was sweating profusely, and the red man, way up above her, was smiling cool, cool. Seeing us grinning at her, Tracy abandoned her task and came over.

"Yep!" she said, panting. "He gay."

"Lord!" I said. "Why?"

We waved at him and his posse and turned to go. And then I felt someone pull my arm from behind. I turned around to face him.

"Yuh leaving aready?" he said.

"Um … yeah …" I said, confused.

"But I didn't get to dance with yuh."

"Well, yuh was dancing with my friend … who stop yuh?" I said.

He looked behind me at Tracy and shook his head.

"No," he said, "I mean, she … my friend was checking yuh … I …"

"Okay," I said, only because he was so damn gorgeous. "Okay. One quick one."

I looked back at Tracy and Jed and mouthed to them to give me five minutes.

And then his arms were on my hips and I turned back to him, not knowing where to look; eventually I put my arms around his waist and, as if inspired, he pulled me closer in to him. I had never danced with someone this tall and it felt weird at first; then our bodies seemed to catch each other's rhythm and we locked into some kind of sexy half-groove, half-wine thing.

And then … music lowering, someone tapping impatiently at my shoulder.

"Got to go," I said, looking up at him.

"Okay," he said, his arms slowly letting me go. "I could call yuh?"

"Sure," I said, turning to go.

"Well," he said, holding my arm and stopping me, "can I get yuh number?"

This time I gave the right number.

"Is Josephine? Right?" he said.

I smiled and nodded, surprised he'd heard, furthermore remembered, my name when I yelled it to him earlier. As I turned around, Tracy was gaping at me. I walked up to her, linked my arm into hers and said, grinning, "He not gay."

"Snake Body" we called him. The six-foot-something red man whose legs just went on and on. We joked that he could slither over us at any time. About a week later he called me. He had the sexiest telephone voice, and when he laughed, shy and easy at the same time, I felt weak. Every damn thing about this man turned me on and I was vexed, because I wanted my space and my freedom, and just like that this man had wriggled his way into my thoughts, and was tempting me to bite the damn apple that had put us women in trouble since the beginning.

Now there were two phone calls I could count on every day: one that left me angry and shouting as Hayden went from platitude to rebuke, and one that left me tingling with the promise that new relationships bring.

One time I had tonsillitis so badly I could barely talk. First Hayden called, suggesting I get some ice-cream, then Snake Body called, saying the same thing. I had barely hung up the phone and crawled back into my bed when the doorbell rang. I looked out of the window and my heart bounced into my stomach then up into my throat. Snake Body was standing by my gate!

And Lord! The man looked even better in the daylight.

"Who's that?" called my mother from inside.

I poked my head into her room.

"No one," I croaked, "just somebody with something. I'll go and get it!"

As I opened the door, I slowed my steps and made myself breathe. Our long driveway leading to the gate seemed even longer. I hoped I looked cool, because, *shit!* I did it again! Raked my eyes over the body lounging, leaning, on my gate. The tight jeans, the navel-breaker, the abs, the abs, the abs … Lord! When I remembered to look up at him and grin, I saw that his eyes were raking over my body too, and I became conscious of my very tight shorts and my legs. I faltered, blushing like a fool. He started to blush too and looked quickly up at me.

"Hi," he said, holding out a parcel. "I brought you some ice-cream."

"Oh." *Jeez!* I opened the gate and took the bag.

"Thanks," I said, intently staring at the parcel in my hand.

"I hope it helps," he said. "I miss talking to yuh."

Shit! "Uh," said the usually-in-control Josephine. I looked up at him and resorted to the grin that had saved me a thousand times.

"Well, thanks," I said again.

"Yuh welcome."

I closed back the gate. I had to get inside; this mooksie Josephine was not the girl I knew.

"Okay, see yuh," I called, turning away.

"Okay, Josephine," he said, and I knew he was watching my ass.

So that's how it happened. Snake Body got to me and I couldn't help myself, yet I wanted my freedom too. Obviously, a situation ripe for trouble. Bit by bit he slithered himself into my life; into my thoughts and plans, and, floored by an immense physical attraction and his shyness, I allowed it to happen. I got real kicks from the effect he had on my friends and the girls at school, for some evenings he would come to pick me up at school and the next day I'd be bombarded with requests for introductions and hopeful queries as to whether he was my brother, to which I always replied "yes". I could see him falling for me, and the old Josephine power returned. But there was something else, too, something I realized early on: this man had the ability to get under my skin. This didn't bother me too much at first, for I was riding high with the confidence and conceit of youth, so I took it in stride and just went with the intense attraction I was feeling.

For all his good looks and the drooling effect he had on women, this man was as nerdy and innocent as they came. Of course, this made him more wanted and sexier. Every woman who met him, including my best friends, all had this fantasy about being the one to break him out. Sex appeal oozed from his pores like cologne, and he didn't have a clue. He reminded me of a girl I used to know.

The first time we kissed was on a Saturday afternoon after we had come from the movies. He hadn't tried to hold my hand in the cinema, or to do the famous yawn and stretch, or anything else. We'd left with Tracy's pronouncement that he was gay reverberating in my ears. But after the show he'd driven up to Sumadh Gardens and parked on the hill, and we had looked down at the city of San Fernando below us and all the lights, and he had asked nerdy things about the view and sea below, till I laughed out loud, and he eventually asked if he could kiss me. This kiss was a complete cross between Paul and Hayden. It was innocent yet demanding; it was passion held back yet toyed with just enough to make it dangerous, yet promising. And it was either the kiss or the height we were at that left me breathless.

After about four months, Snake Body and I started going steady. Without my even realizing, he'd wiped out the competition. I was floored by his ease, his sexiness, his quietness, the way he could be shy yet sure. He moved into a space that I had forgotten about, the space where the old, sweet, innocent Josephine lived. Snake Body had found his way inside me. Everything I had boxed in and sealed, he pulled out, dusted off and gently pried open the lid. I found myself revealing hurts I hadn't known I still remembered, telling stories that surprised even me. Slowly, he peeled the mask of cool confidence off and revealed what lay hidden beneath.

Always before I had gone for the ones with 'trouble' stamped all over them, excited by the power I had over these seeming Casanovas; now the one that looked safe was proving to be the most dangerous to me. Though for a while after we started going steady I continued to move like a single girl, to flirt and lime and throw Snake Body off when he wasn't around with the same ease I'd done the others, something nagged me inside. Not guilt, but a feeling that something bigger than I could fathom was happening here. With everything he did and said, Snake Body moved closer and closer into my well-guarded space. And because this space was not consciously created, and I couldn't tell it was being invaded, I became more confused. All I could feel was some Josephine-something seeping out, or clearing away to reveal something else, and I wanted to run and I wanted to stay.

The first time Snake Body invited me to his house was another story. His house was old and big and rambling, with a massive yard that held dogs and horses and gamecocks and cats. I felt as if I'd been swept into one of my favourite Enid Blyton childhood stories. And as I came through the door, a short, plump woman, with two plaits and the biggest smile I'd ever seen, walked straight up to me and enveloped me in a hug so complete I laughed aloud. And, just like that, Snake Body's mother pulled me more into him.

When he kissed me and touched me, I tingled, not just my body, but my inside. His kisses made me feel warm with something akin to heat, yet innocent. And the first time we made love it was sweet and sexy and urgent and gentle all at the same time. Something happened to me when his body was on top me, inside me, like I could no longer tell where he ended and where I began. I felt like a woman and a child and a virgin and a whore all wrapped into one, and it wasn't about expertise, no, this sex was something else, something not just physical.

My friends told me I was in love. They laughed and teased me: the Untouchable Josephine, finally … succumbed! While I laughed along with them, something inside me was more than a little afraid and angry. Who was he to come and wrap himself around me like this? Who was he to make me lose control? Why was I giving up so much of myself to him? When I was with James I was happy, but away from him, I pondered these questions and reached for the Josephine who could compartmentalize herself so easily.

With little attention paid to my work, I somehow obtained one of the top five A Level passes at school. With this confidence in my abilities and looks, I sailed into UWI the following year, so caught up in the nothingness that we often create to forget the truth, I'd forgotten going to UWI was not my desire. Flippantly I enrolled without giving my degree much thought, and my coolness that had drawn others to me before brought them again. Within the second week, I found myself in hot demand for all-fours games. The next week, the Guild of Undergraduates wanted me as a peer counsellor, and by the end of the month everyone thought I was having a hot affair with Robert, the Guild President. And the more James tapped on my shoulder for me to take notice, the more I shrugged him off.

Every weekend I went to some UWI fete or the other. If James couldn't come, too bad. I went with my friends. He didn't complain at first, just suggested that we could spend some time alone, that I should come down South. I ignored him, and then one weekend he refused to come. I shrugged it off and went about the business of feting, but I didn't have such a great time as I pretended to. And when I called his house the next day and he sounded far too distant even for South, and said he didn't think this was working out, it was like a giant cloud suddenly burst over me. Of course my friends didn't hesitate to say the cloud had been threatening all along, I'd just refused to see it, but this didn't stop me from reeling. How could he break up with me just like that? Who did he think he was? So ego and I rode down South that weekend and demanded that Snake Body make up with me. And he refused.

I went through the motions of living, but something more than my ego was rattled, something deep inside me, boxed and hidden away, some memory of loss. Things that had come naturally to me before, like enjoyment, now required concentration. I was barely putting one foot in front of the other and managing to grin, when one of my housemates, Simone, died.

"Hang Jack in yuh pweffen!" shouted Derrick, slapping his ace down on the table as he jumped up.

We grinned at each other.

"Nice game, partner!" I said, high-fiving him across the table.

"This getting boring, Jo We have to go by the junction and see if we could find some people to play us a good game of all-fours," he said, pushing back his chair and faking a yawn.

"Oh, shut up!" said Jay, packing up the cards and steupsing.

"Hi, guys," said Simone, coming in and flopping down on the mattress that served as a couch. She threw her books on the ground and closed her eyes, pressed her fingers to her head. "God, I have a headache," she said.

"You want some Panadol?" I asked.

She nodded.

By night-time she had used up my two packs of Panadol and her headache had not gone. But, since we were invincible youth, we paid little attention.

Two days later, her birthday, the headache still had not gone.

She came in from class, looking weary. We sat at the table, pretending to play all-fours, ignoring her.

"Well, hello ..." she said, looking from one to the other, wondering that we could forget her birthday.

"Oh, hi," we said, barely looking up from the cards.

She hung around a while, then went into the room. We snickered among ourselves and then, after about ten minutes, we ran inside, jumped on the bed and showered her with hugs and kisses. Later that night, we chipped in and treated her to dinner at a Chinese restaurant we frequented for its cheap food and large specials, and though she laughed and talked, her continuous squinting, the way she winced and touched her forehead, made us worried enough that we forced her to go home the next day and see her doctor.

By the weekend, Simone was in hospital. I went four days later to see her; legs buckling on me, remembering another time, I could only stare at her fingernails that she painted and filed every night, now poking out from those awful white sheets like yellow talons. She could barely move her head as she gave me a weak smile. I left the room in tears. When the phone rang a couple of days later, I knew, even before Derrick told me, that Simone was dead. Meningitis.

We hugged each other and cried, shocked by the suddenness and speed of it all, as if life had just fast-forwarded on us while we were still on slow, easy groove. Everywhere in the tiny house we shared were signs of her – make-up, endless bottles of nail polish, clothes – each time we looked around and realized she wasn't here we looked at each other in shock. The shaking inside me grew.

I had barely made it through her funeral when another friend from campus, Lynton, died. Shy, quiet Lynton, the only one of the fellas who used to sit on the bench, checking out the assets of campus, that I talked to, because I could see so much kindness in his eyes. He'd gone to a fete over the weekend and, like everyone else, he'd partied in the rain. But on Wednesday morning, he alone was dead. Pneumonia this time.

An old forgotten memory reverberated within me, surprising me with its force as if it had happened yesterday. A memory of another time, a long tedious flight of stairs, a corridor, a room full of pain and false promises and regrets never acknowledged. I pulled back in horror, seeing a sad and frightened girl who I had thought was gone forever. A girl whose eyes pulled me in the mirror, asking, *Does death hit the young too? In the midst of our laughing and waking and living?* Way inside, another voice rebuked, *After joy comes sorrow.* I began to shake with uncertainty.

Cleo

Cleo and I were having one of our usual fights; this time it was the day before my Common Entrance Exam. We were scraping, biting, cuffing and flinging insults at each other. This fight had the space to flourish into full scale war because our mother, who usually got us off the battlefield by turning her own weaponry against one or both of us, was downstairs chatting with a friend. With no one to intervene, we moved in for the kill.

Finding my nails no match for Cleo's talons, I gathered a mouthful of spit and waited till she moved in to scrape. With great accuracy, I aimed my spittle ball straight into her eye. She screamed – a piercing, blood-curdling sound, in whose wake only silence could follow.

And then, "Mummy! Mummy! Josephine spit on me! Mummmmmmmmy!"

She ran out of the back door and down the steps, screaming for my mother, while I ran behind her to defend myself against whatever lies she would tell.

I will never forget the look on my mother's face as we came down the stairs. She looked up from her chair, her face a terrible sea of anger and embarrassment that she hid poorly with a sideways smile. Her friend stared agape at us. Retreat would of course have been the most sensible way to end the war, but neither Cleo nor I was lucid enough to pay heed.

"Josephine spit on me, I say!" screamed Cleo.

"She scrape me and bite me!" I shouted.

"Yuh lie! Yuh spit …"

"Okay. Okay, girls," said our mother, her smile tightening. "When I come inside."

"No! No! I not taking that! Do something!" said Cleo, crying.

"Is you she have to do something!" I shouted.

"I said," our mother stood up, "when I come inside."

"Nora, I better go," said Mummy's friend, also standing. "These girls like they need some straightening out."

"No, Yvonne, you sit down," said Mummy. "Go inside, girls."

I turned and stamped back upstairs, seeing Cleo open her mouth to argue, even as Mummy turned away from her with a warning look.

Inside, we glared at each other as enemies revealed. I got my book bag and sat at the table, trying to do homework, but seething inside, while Cleo stamped down the corridor with the force of an ogre, and went into our room.

As if she could see outside, Cleo was waiting for our mother by the back door when she came up the steps.

"What yuh going to do Josephine?" she demanded of Mummy as she came through the doorway.

Mummy ignored her, headed down the corridor and to her bedroom.

Behind her, Cleo shouted, "Yuh just going to leave her? Let her spit on me? She always getting away with all kinda thing, eh! If was me do that!"

And then Mummy's voice, cold and deathly.

"Listen! Just leave me alone, yuh hear! All yuh embarrass me, yuh hear! Shame me! Everybody going to go and say how Miss Chin children can't behave!"

"That's all yuh does study! 'People this, people that.' Josephine spit on me and yuh talking 'bout 'people'!" Cleo was shouting at the top of her voice now, while I pretended to study at the dining table.

"Yuh does never do her nothing! She could get away with anything!" screamed Cleo.

Now I jumped up. "That's a lie! Is you always starting thing with me! It good! It good I spit on yuh!"

"Yuh hear? Yuh hear her? 'It good'. Yuh hear her, Mummy?"

"It good, oui!"

And then a far more angry voice than either of ours rose and prevailed.

"Shut up! Shut up, both of you! I fed up of this damn stupidness!" Mummy screamed from her bedroom.

And then I heard Cleo start again, "Now yuh …" and she stopped.

And I looked up from my books in time to see Mummy charging down the corridor like a mad bull. Charging straight up to me. Into me.

And I was still looking up at her, wondering what was going on, when the first thwack of the wooden hanger slammed into my legs. The shock of its sting made me jump up, giving my mother more acreage, and she wasted no time. The hanger stung my legs, back, arms.

"Oh God!" I screamed, "Oh God!", jumping from leg to leg, covering and rubbing aching body parts as Mummy's hanger ruthlessly moved to uncovered areas.

And then, another voice – a voice that cried with the pain I felt – shouted, desperately, "Run! Run, Jo! Run!"

I looked towards this sound, this strange sound of Cleo, calling for me, feeling for me. Saving me.

"Run!" she screamed at me, tears pouring down her face, as she held up over her head Mummy's favourite vase.

Mummy spun away from me to the sound behind her; hanger poised in the air, she screamed at Cleo, "Put that down! Put it down!"

"Run, Jo!" screamed Cleo, and then, to Mummy, "I will break it! I will break it, yuh hear? Leave her! Run, Jo!"

I gaped from one enemy to the next, totally confused.

"Put that down!" shouted Mummy again, as she began moving towards Cleo.

Cleo's arms above her head shook, her eyes opened wider, prompting action from me.

"Run!" she screamed.

As Mummy moved into Cleo, I ran. I ran past Cleo, out the back door, down the steps, with Mummy shouting behind me, "Come back here!" and then, "Yuh little wretch!"

"Yes!" said Cleo. "Kill me now!"

At the bottom of the steps I heard the hanger whip skin again, and then the sound of the vase as it crashed to the floor, its shattering reaching into every nerve in my body, and I shook violently, inside and out.

Cleo, of all people, sensed something of what was going on with me. She came to UWI one weekend and tried to talk to me. One of her friends had died as a teenager and she knew how bewildered I felt. She had touched my hand one morning at the table and said softly, "Josephine, yuh want to talk about it?"

"What?" I said, hiding as I did so often, behind flippancy.

"You know – Simone, and yuh other friend. I know when Michael had died … yuh know … how we were feeling."

"Oh!" I said. "No. No. I all right."

Cleo had stared at me, trying to get inside me, and I had resorted to the Josephine grin.

"Really," I said, "I'm fine."

"Oh. Okay," Cleo shrugged, and as she got up, immediately I wanted to pull her back down, to grab her and cry and tell her that I really wasn't all right. Instead, I looked up at her with a stupid grin and let the moment pass.

Because it was only on the inside; this trembling. Outside, Josephine showed the appropriate reaction, bounced back in the appropriate time, no one knew of the Josephine who began sneaking peeps behind her, just to make sure Sister Angelica or the Devil, or Daddy, or Death, didn't pounce. No one saw the Josephine who held on with sweaty palms and gritting teeth and baited breath to the truth that everyone left. No one knew that Josephine had started reining back in that spirit, the spirit that was not enough to stop the bad things from happening.

Only when I was alone I would find myself suddenly unable to breathe, or hear my heart beating with such ferocity I felt it would come out of my chest, and I would jump up and pace, fearing that sitting still would bring something bad, fearing that I wasn't looking out enough, ready enough, just in case.

One night I was going out with Jessie, worrying that I'd see James and his new woman there, when I began to feel the car closing in on me. I could feel the space around me getting smaller, I could feel my heart thudding inside my chest, my hands sweating, I was dizzy, I couldn't breathe.

"Jessie," I said, "stop the car."

I got out and started to pace the pavement.

"What happen, Jo?" asked Jessie.

"I doh know. I feeling weird."

"Like what?" she said, stopping my pacing by holding my arm. Her eyes pierced into mine.

"I doh know," I said again. "Suppose I dying."

"How yuh could be dying just so?"

"I doh know!" I snapped.

"Yuh want to go to the hospital?" she asked.

I shook my head hard. Hospitals were deceivers. They gave false hope. Took away the living. Took from the living.

"No," I said, "I want to go home."

"Okay," she said. "Okay, let's go."

We went back to her house. I stumbled inside and lay down. Unknown to me, Jessie called the family doctor.

She came in shortly after with some Coke.

"Dr Ram say yuh blood sugar fell. Drink this."

I took the Coke and sipped, upset that I had Jessie so worried. Now that I was home I was feeling a lot better. Eventually, with Jessie rubbing my head, I fell asleep.

When UWI closed for vacation and I came South, I found myself talking to James every day on the phone. Once I started talking about Lynton and Simone and I broke down on the phone, my heart started to race and I could barely talk between my sobs.

"James," I said, "I have to go."

I hung up the phone and dashed into my room. Lying on my bed, I could feel and hear my heart so much I swore I was having a heart attack right there. I jumped back up and went outside to sit on the swing, whose rocking eventually gave me a different rhythm to focus on. Just as I began to feel my heart slowing down, a car pulled up to our gate.

"James!" I said smiling and jumping up, remembering that sweet man who'd brought me ice-cream when I needed it. But it wasn't James. It was someone to my mother. I went upstairs to call her and then I dialled James.

"I feeling better," I said.

"Oh, good," he said.

"I … thought yuh would have come," I said.

"Oh." Silence. Then, "I really didn't think of it, Josephine."

"Oh."

Still, a few weeks later we made up, neither of us believing the changes in each other, each of us thinking we could fix it. Months later, lying in bed by James, watching television with him, I sat up with this horrible feeling inside me. I jumped off the bed so violently that he sat up.

"Wha's the matter, Josephine?" he said.

"I … I doh know," I said, pacing.

The room was spinning, I could barely breathe.

"Josephine," he said, "come and sit down."

"No, no, I can't."

He got up, came to stand in front me, pulled me to his chest. I fiddled and pushed him away, needing to keep moving. He held me firmly, forced me back to the bed.

"Close yuh eyes," he said, pulling me to him. He rubbed my back with slow circles. I could feel my body resisting the impulse to relax that had come over it.

"Take a deep breath," he said, "hold it while I count."

The sound of his voice and the rubbing of my back gradually got to me. I felt my shoulders relax until, eventually, my body slumped against his.

"Wha's wrong with me, James?" I whispered.

"Shhh," he said, stroking my head.

139

Eventually, I relaxed.

This of course made things worse. Now he became my safe zone, the one who could fix it. Once he was there, I'd be all right. The fear and flippancy that had ruled my life for so long now became my prison. I made James my crutch; if I loved him it was related to needing him. If I did not need him, would I love him?

Part Three

Grounded

"I no longer creep, 'cause I've learnt to use my feet, can't yet run, 'cause the journey's just begun, but I'll get there … Walking."

Josephine Chin

Candlefly

✸

I graduated from UWI, miraculously, with Honours, and then I ended up, guess where? Teaching.

Against my better judgement I'd come back South to live after graduating, even though I hated San Fernando, having fallen in love with St Augustine and Port of Spain. But I had also fallen in love with James – now my husband – who was a die-hard Southerner. I came back down knowing I was going to be bored and miserable here. St Augustine had provided the anonymity I craved; South would always see me as another Chin. Yet, I'd been following other people's decisions for my life for so long I no longer knew when I was doing what I wanted and when I wasn't.

My first teaching appointment sent me even further South, to a place I'd only heard of but never imagined: Moruga.

Unlike my older sisters who had been born in various country areas, I was the only one who was born and bred a city girl; now here was city girl heading to the most country of country. The late Dr Eric Williams had once been known to say, "If Trinidad was a donkey, Moruga would be its tail"; whether this was because Moruga was behind God's back or because it forever tailed Trinidad and never caught up, I didn't know, but I would find out soon enough.

James took me down the first day of school. I felt like the perfect teacher, full of UWI knowledge, dressed up sharp in a new skirt-suit that was both young and professional, armed with the knowledge of Moruga's poverty and backwardness. I was going to make a difference.

From the time we passed Cowen Hamilton High School in Princes Town, the last frontier of civilization, I felt it.

"Yuh feel that?" I asked James.

"What?" he said, his eyes intent on the snaking road before us.

"Like, I doh know, like a curtain fall."

"How yuh mean?" he said, briefly glancing at me with a puzzled expression.

"I doh know, is like if a curtain fall behind us, a shadow, something …"

He shook his head and smiled.

"God! Josephine, you dramatic, eh? This is Princes Town or something. Anyway, we nearly reach."

The road wound to the left then to the right, reminding me of those tree-shrouded country roads I used to get sick on as a child, when we went for Sunday evening drives. After some time, we saw a road sign welcoming us to Moruga.

"Thank God!" said James. "I was wondering when we going to reach."

"How long we driving for now?"

He glanced at the clock on the dashboard.

"About an hour," he said.

"God, yuh mean I have to take this kinda drive every day!"

"You'll get used to it, I suppose."

We drove on in silence. Ten minutes. Another ten minutes.

"But where this school is in truth?" said James eventually.

"You sure we didn't pass it?" I asked.

He shook his head.

"Ask somebody, nah."

He ignored me. I looked at the clock anxiously. No way could I be late on my first day. I turned to the window, looking out for someone to ask for directions. Eventually I saw an old man pushing a bicycle up the road.

"Morning," I said, poking my head out of the window. "We looking for the school, Moruga Composite."

"Yuh nearly there, keep going a lil bit," he said, grinning at me with a toothless mouth.

"See?" said James. "I tell yuh we didn't pass it."

"Yeah, right," I said.

We drove on.

And on.

"Lord," I said, "I doh think I could take this drive every day, nah."

"They real put this school in the bush, boy," said James, exasperated.

Looking out of the window I saw some women filling buckets by a standpipe.

"Where the school?" I asked them.

They stared back at me like I was talking a different language.

"Composite," I said a little louder, "Moruga Composite."

One of the women lifted her arm and pointed, looking at me as if I was stupid.

Following her direction I saw it, a sign between some trees and a narrow road to the right, slightly inclined, leading into the school. Scores of students in cream and red uniforms stood by a little parlour at the bottom of the road. Apparently oblivious to the fact that it was five minutes before the bell, they laughed and joked and hailed out to others who were crawling in off the road.

It didn't take me long to realize that ranting with my students about this tardiness was not going to work. They would stare back at me blankly.

"Why worry, Miss?"

"Wha's the big deal, Miss?"

"Wha's the fuss about, Miss?"

145

And because their questions showed genuine puzzlement, I couldn't shake the feeling that I was missing something big here.

My form class was a group of Form Threes who I soon fell in love with. They in turn regarded me with great curiosity, awe and amusement: 'The Big-City Miss With A UWI Degree'. I found myself up against an invisible wall as big words like Emancipation and Progress seemed to have little if any meaning here.

As my confidence in academia wavered, I found myself bewildered. The few pairs of interested eyes in the sea of boredom that faced me every day were not enough to keep me going. I found I was not the type of teacher who could "teach a few and ignore the rest", as my peers advised me to do in order to keep my sanity. Unlike my young teachers at Convent who had had the advantages of intellectualism and interest among their students, so that little was required of them other than teaching, I found that teaching was the thing least required of me. Inventiveness, motivation and counselling were my top priority. In fact, I could not teach without putting these things in place, and so I became consumed with finding new ways of imparting knowledge, and often this knowledge did not come from the textbooks.

So instead of teaching my students the dates and places of Columbus's arrival in the West Indies, I had them tell me about the annual re-enactment of Discovery Day that took place in Moruga, an event which they attended yearly and sometimes participated in, without any understanding of its historical roots. And instead of telling them about our ethnic heritage, I called out the many African names of students, and had them tell me about the place names in Moruga, so many of which reflect the French heritage of our island. And when all else failed with about five boys in my class, and they refused to behave, I gained permission to take them on a trip to the San Fernando court and holding-place for criminals. Without consciously knowing what I was doing, my efforts began to make education a practical thing, and I noticed, when I had these students for first period, that they eventually stopped dragging into school and would instead be waiting in class for me when I got there.

But I was still challenged by a few who would, without fail, have their heads on the desk every Wednesday when I had them after lunch. After quarrelling and tapping them on many occasions, I eventually asked wearily one day, "Why all yuh in this mess every Wednesday?"

Grudgingly they sat up, eyes mixed with defiance and boredom.

"I want to know why," I said. "I want to put an end to this."

A snicker passed through the class.

"What so funny?" I asked.

Silence.

I pushed my chair back and crossed my legs.

"I can wait all day for an answer, yuh know," I said to them. "I can't be the only one making an effort here. And I can't help if I don't know what's going on."

I could feel the confusion in the class, as they looked at one another. Eventually, braver and bolder than the rest, Ron stood up.

"Hungry, Miss," he said, without looking at me.

"What?" I said, sure I'd heard wrong. "What yuh say?"

Now he looked up at me, his eyes challenging mine.

"I say they hungry, Miss."

"But … you just had lunch …"

"No." This was said in a flat, dead chorus.

"It was just lunchtime …" I said, confused.

"That doh mean we had lunch," someone muttered.

I stared at them, feeling foolish.

The whole lunch hour, the dragging into school in the mornings, the anxious eyes on the clock during last period, all these things suddenly made sense to me.

"Yuh mean …" I said softly, "yuh mean all yuh don't eat for the whole day in school?"

"Sometimes," said Paul – a tall, strong boy, whose sad eyes had melted my heart the first time I saw him – "sometimes we eat and sometimes we doh eat."

Now those eyes challenged me to dare pity him.

I stared at him, looked around at the class, now seeing them; more drawn to some than the others, always careful not to show it, held in check by a lifetime of memories. Finally I said, hiding my shock with efficiency, "Well, why didn't somebody tell me?"

Laughter shot through the class like bamboo bursting.

"What so funny?" I asked angrily.

"So, Miss," said Ron, grinning, "what yuh will do, feed the whole class?"

"If I have to," I said, standing now in front of him.

Slowly his grin moved down his face till it disappeared. The class gaped at me.

"Right, so now this sorted out, turn to page eleven."

They sent him the next day to test my word. And when, in shock, he finally took the three dollars I handed him for lunch, Ron looked up at me with the most incredulous expression on his face. The next day there were three students. The next day, four. By the end of the week, I'd given lunch money out every day.

The teachers started teasing me.

"Miss, take care they break yuh, yuh know."

"Miss, doh worry with them, they good smart yuh know."

"Miss, yuh give Maleka money? That miserable child?"

"So that mean she not entitled to eat?" I retorted angrily.

But their words plagued me. I began to wonder if I was being played for a fool.

Not knowing what else to do, I prayed about it that night. The next day it came to me at school. Instead of giving money, I would set up an account with Miss Joan, the lady who ran the cafeteria. That way I would be sure the students really used the money for food, and I wouldn't have to worry about running out of cash. I told Miss Joan to give only lunch, no snacks, and I would pay her at the end of the month. The result was that the jokers could no longer use the facility and the ones who were too embarrassed to ask could eat without my knowing.

Most of the teachers laughed. They told me the students would resent my playing big shot. They told me to pick out the one or two who really needed it, for a couple of them did provide lunches for one or two students in their Form classes. But I decided it was not up to me to decide who should and who shouldn't be fed.

At the end of the month, however, I was seriously reconsidering my decision. My lunch bill was two hundred dollars. I was angry, because this was way over what I had calculated; did the students think I was soft for true?

I could see the students regarding me, assessing me, discussing whether or not I would continue as promised. Without meaning to, I ended up during one of my Monday Morning Motivation talks, talking about honesty and integrity.

"In the end, what makes a man or a woman great is how much each stands for the truth," I said, "how honourable he is, how he remains right, even when no one is looking."

Looks of guilt passed around the class. I could feel a pulse beating in the room, an unspoken message being relayed, as eyes that met mine glinted with a sudden something.

By the end of that month, the bill had gone down to one hundred dollars, and it never again rose beyond that amount.

And another development took place. I began finding bags on my desk; bags laden with fruit: mango, pommecythere, chennet, whatever fruit was in season. Some days the bags would spill onto the floor. Bewildered, I would ask in the staffroom where the bags had come from, but few teachers would meet my eyes, and all replied with shrugs.

I never saw the students put the bags there. But I understood that my students were giving back, were saying *Thank you*, and their self-respect made those gifts priceless to me.

Now the knowledge that they could give back to me infused them with an even greater power, and they set out now to teach me, to educate me; and what could they know that 'City Miss' didn't? What everybody in Moruga knows, of course – obeah.

Hearing that I didn't believe in obeah, my Form class set out to teach me different. One Monday, after a particularly hard weekend of partying with my husband, the morning found me looking tired and washed up, and no matter what I told my students they were convinced that the root of my tiredness was my husband's playing the fool. They set about giving me the recipe for 'stay home', guaranteed to make a playing, straying husband turn into a docile home-pet. Lily swore her mother had done this and that since then her mother could get away with anything with her husband, including bringing her horner-man home. Another student swore her aunt had captured another woman's husband by giving him sweat rice to eat.

I laughed heartily at these anecdotes.

"So what about love?" I asked. "Why isn't love enough?"

"Love, Miss?" said Paul. "What is that?"

"Love does die, Miss," said Laverne.

"And fade away," said Leah.

"Play yuh studying love, Miss, see if somebody doh work obeah on yuh husband and take him 'way," said Ron.

I shook my head and laughed.

"Imagine young people like all yuh so superstitious!" I said.

The class laughed too.

150

"Doh worry, Miss, yuh go see for yuhself," promised Bevin.

"Stay in Moruga long enough, Miss, yuh go believe in obeah," predicted Paul.

Though I continued to laugh, the whole obeah thing was piquing my curiosity. I have always been fascinated by the supernatural; now that I was in the midst of obeah country itself, I was determined to find out all I could. I started asking all my classes about obeah. They offered to take me to meet Mother Cocksburn, who many swore was the most powerful obeah woman in the country. Even the big-boy politicians went to her, my students told me. She could 'see' for me, they said, and would tell me who to look out for and how to protect myself; they swore her obeah cast spells that transcended generations. She was even reported to have worked obeah on Papa Neeza, a powerful obeah man, because he had removed a spell she had put on someone.

One day in my Fourth Form history class, inspiration hit. It was always like pulling teeth to get my class to do the School Based Assessments required for passing the CXC exam. Suddenly enlightened, I assigned them to do a study of how religious influences affect societal culture. They could expound about obeah on this topic. It was the first SBA I got on time and the grades were excellent. I found out, years later, that the Caribbean Examinations Council had used my assignment as a case study on how to bring history to life and how to use it to encourage students to have a greater understanding of their environment.

Reading and correcting the SBAs only fuelled my curiosity more. One day I brought the subject up in the staffroom.

"Everything down here is 'obeah', eh?" I said. "I can't believe these children believe in obeah like this."

Silence.

Then Miss Jones turned to me, her face dead serious.

"Obeah is true thing, oui. I doh make joke 'bout that again, nah."

"You too, miss?" I said, shocked. "A born and bred city girl like yuhself?"

"City girl have nothing to do with it, nah. I working here long enough to know obeah is true thing, yes."

I laughed.

"Doh laugh nah, miss. That is good talk," said Mr Mangroo.

"You too, sir?" I said, turning to him. "Jeez, all yuh sounding like the students."

"Tell her about Judy, nah," said Miss Gomez, poking Miss Jones.

Miss Jones cut her eyes at her and shook her head.

"Who is Judy?" I asked.

No one answered me.

"Come, nah. Who is Judy?"

"Yuh sure yuh want to hear?" Miss Jones asked.

"Yes. Sure," I said eagerly.

She stared at me intently.

"Judy was in my Form Class last year," she finally said, "a real bright girl. And then she start doing bad in school, doing no homework, that kind of thing …"

"Obeah, right?" I said, grinning.

"Shhhhhh!" Chorus.

"Anyway," said Miss Jones, "one day I pull her aside and ask her what going on. She tell me her mother have a next man. She say her mother went by Mother Lenny and get something that have her father so dotish she bringing the outside man home, in his face and he can't do nothing."

I was still amused but I kept the smile off my face. The mood had changed in the staffroom, I could feel it like a cloud or something heavy in the air. I shuddered. It was the exact same feeling I got every morning as I passed Cowen Hamilton High School and began the road to Moruga.

"Anyway, this went on for weeks. I even went to see her mother to tell her how Judy work falling, but she wasn't home and the father was no use to talk to. For weeks I watching this child wasting time in school, this child who was so bright. I talking to her and she not taking me on. She pick up with some fella and that make things worse. Every night she going Princes Town with him to lime. Eventually, somebody convince the father to go by Papa Neeza, somebody convince him is obeah working on him. And he didn't want to believe that could happen to him, because he was a big police in Moruga, macho man with plenty rank. Anyway, he went by Papa Neeza, who tell him to buy a dress for the wife and bring it for him."

Everyone was spellbound now. Including me.

"So he buy the dress, and he carry it by the obeah man, and Papa Neeza tell him make sure nobody but his wife put it on first, hang it up in the cupboard when he reach home and take the wife out that night and make her wear it. So the father went home and hang the dress up and sit up waiting for his wife to come home, till he fall asleep waiting for her, and is Judy come home and put on the dress instead and gone out with her boyfriend. A couple of months later we notice Judy like she getting fat. I pull her aside one day and ask her what going on. She tell me 'Nothing.' 'Yuh pregnant?' I say. 'No, Miss, no,' she tell me, but I doh believe her. Next thing Judy start to faint in class and running outside to vomit. I ask her again, still she tell me no. One day she get so sick we had to take her to Princes Town Clinic and they send her straight to San'do Hospital. Guess what?"

"She pregnant," I say.

"No." A chorus.

"No," said Miss Jones, "she not pregnant. In fact, they can't find what wrong with her. They say they have to keep her a while, and all the time, the chile belly only swelling."

"Swelling?" I said, incredulous. "How yuh mean swelling?"

"Swelling," she said. "Every day it bigger and bigger, and then she start to smell bad."

"Bad? Bad how?" I asked.

"Like … like she rotting."

I rocked back in my chair and held my nose. I could smell the smell she was talking about, that hopeless, all consuming smell. The smell of death. My pores raised.

"Eventually they tell her mother come for her, they can't do nothing. By now her belly big like if she's nine months' pregnant and she smelling real bad. By the time she come home, she come on Tuesday, and by Friday she was dead. Her belly bust."

"Nah!" I said, sitting up. I felt sick and weak. "Yuh sure this story true?"

"Too true," said Miss Gomez. "The father went mad after."

"How her belly could just buss?" I asked.

"It just buss," said Miss Jones. "She was dead by Friday morning. So yuh see me, Miss, I don't mess with obeah after that."

I rose to go to the ladies. I had to get out of there, the air seemed to pulse with energy, and now, for the first time since beginning my quest for knowledge on obeah, I was truly afraid. So afraid in fact, that I left it alone after that.

I got a great shock when Millie, one of my quietest, mousiest students, came to school with an enormous hickey on her neck. I called her aside at break time.

"Millie," I said, "I worried about yuh."

"Why, Miss?" she asked, not looking at me.

"Yuh … yuh have a boyfriend, now?" I said.

"No, Miss."

"No? Well what is that on yuh neck?"

Her eyes shifted, her hand covered her neck.

"That is nothing, Miss. That is not no boyfriend."

She looked away, sullen. I had never seen her display this kind of behaviour.

"Look, Millie," I said, reaching out to touch her hand, "I just worried, okay?"

She pulled away.

"Nothing to worry 'bout, Miss." Then, "I could go now?"

I watched her walk away, seeing a boldness in her step I hadn't seen before. Every step she took said, *I am a woman now*. Despite her attitude, I kept pulling her aside, giving her the sex and pregnancy talks I beleaguered my classes with. I kept a constant eye on her. There was something about her I couldn't quite put my finger on. As if she was ashamed and proud at the same time. Yet as she started failing every test and breaking class, she came to school neater and neater – new sneakers, new shirt and skirt – and despite her nonchalance about school, there was a pride about something. This confidence and shame bothered me. Eventually, I went to see her mother.

"She giving yuh trouble?" asked the mother when I said I was worried about Millie.

"No. No, not really."

"Well, wha's the problem, Miss?"

"Well, is just that … I worry about her with boys and thing, yuh know?"

"Miss," said her mother, putting her hands out, placating me, "what yuh want me to do?"

"Maybe we could talk to her together. Talk about sex, getting pregnant …"

"Listen, Miss. I have plenty work to do. I doh know what yuh want me do 'bout Millie."

She heaved herself off the tired old couch we were sitting on. She stared at me and I knew it was time for me to go.

"Millie is a bright girl," I said hurriedly. "I want to see her get her education …"

"Education?" her mother sneered. Arms on her hips she turned to face me with such venom, I pulled back.

"What yuh telling me 'bout education, Miss? What education does do for people? What education will do for she?"

"Well, she could get a job, bring in some money, is the only way …"

"Miss," said her mother, flopping back into the couch, "Miss." She looked at me and shook her head. "I have eight chirren. Millie is the oldest one. Yuh think I could wait for she to get education? She have to see 'bout she self now. I done seeing 'bout she."

I stared at the mother. My mouth dropped open. Surely she couldn't mean … she wasn't saying …

"All I want Millie make sure is that she doh go with no stupidy man, or with no lil boy who can't do nothing for she. All I tell she is find somebody good, with good job, like a police or something, so he could see 'bout she."

I stood up. My legs shaking. I backed out of the house, unable to look at the mother as I left.

In January the endless empty desks in my classes astounded me. After every roll call I realized my boys were disappearing by the dozen.

"Where is Paul?" I asked one day. "And Bevin and Jamieson and Kyle?"

"Hunting, Miss," someone said.

"Hunting?" I said, sure I'd heard wrong.

"Now is hunting season," someone said patiently.

"So yuh mean, these lil fellas gone hunting?" I asked.

The students grinned at me.

"Miss feel we small, yes."

"You are," I said, "you are, what … fourteen, fifteen. What they doing hunting? Where?"

"In the forest, Miss."

"Why? With who?" I was baffled.

"Uncle, father, brother, neighbour, whoever …"

"But," I stammered, "but what about school?"

"School? School doh have no money in it, Miss."

My boys came back two, three months later, tired, manly, and I fought to put them back into their school uniforms, back into learning, back into securing a future, but for many the present was too all-encompassing to see beyond.

Moruga shocked my consciousness – like the tiny, unassuming candlefly that suddenly darts in front of us and flashes us some light, making us only then aware that we are in the dark. Never again will I be confident in what I know; always, I will be looking to learn what I don't. Sometimes I remember so many of those Moruga eyes, those sad, tired, old, too-wise eyes, eyes that, for a moment, I could bring to life, eyes I would see glimmer, jump up, awake into something, a view, of what could be. Sometimes I wonder if I did right to do that, if taking them to the window and showing them outside may have caused them more grief than if they were left to continue believing the world was in this little, tiny room. Sometimes I wonder if I, too, should have been a candlefly, or if I should have left them in the dark.

To me, Moruga is the colour of hope erased, the ignorance of minds so rich in the past that tomorrow is an impossibility, the colonization of culture that shrouds it in mystery and fear still, rather than in knowledge and pride; yet, too, it is the power of survival, the truth of man's strength and flexibility and innovation, and I wish so much that these students who gave me a new meaning to the term 'street wise and city smart' would wonder at and revel in who they are, enough to pull them into who they could be.

The Promise

As first pregnancies go, I was filled with a naivety and overwhelmed by the prospect. I thought, as the books tell us, that pregnancy and motherhood were going to be this wonderful experience. While I was ecstatic at first, I could not ignore the growing restlessness inside me. As my stomach grew, so did my doubts, my questions, my thoughts. People thought the quietness I exuded was a pensiveness about the enormity of my upcoming new role. I myself had no explanation of what it was; all I knew was that something inside me needed addressing. As the time drew nearer to have my baby, I began to get desperate; I needed this something inside me fixed before my baby came, so that I would not be so distracted and would be able to come into motherhood at my best.

One day, as I was talking to a friend on the phone, she said, "You must be so excited, eh? Can't wait, eh?"

"Yes," I said, hesitant to reveal this nameless thing that I felt so intensely, this confusion, "I am …"

"What?" she said, hearing me falter.

"Is just … I doh know, I can't really say."

"Nervous. Is nervous yuh nervous."

"Yuh think?" I said hopefully, glad for this simple explanation.

"Yeah. Yuh want to make sure yuh do it right."

As she said this, I jumped. "What yuh mean?" I asked, offended without knowing why.

"I doh know … just, yuh want to do it right …" she said.

"But," I said, "I mean, all new mothers want to. Everybody want to do it right. What make me any different?"

"I doh mean the basic things, I mean the big things ... the things you didn't have ..." she mumbled in the end.

Something inside me jumped.

"How yuh know what I had or didn't have?" I said angrily.

"Josephine," she said, "doh get vex, is just ... yuh know, yuh mother was strict and you yuhself say yuh couldn't talk nothing 'bout boyfriend and thing. Maybe is just, yuh working out what kinda mother yuh want to be, what yuh will change and what yuh will keep."

The woolly head I'd been walking around with for I don't know how long, suddenly cleared.

I suddenly understood that I had a choice. That it was up to me. That I was in control.

When the contractions finally came, I was so quiet everyone thought I was scared.

"No sense worrying now," said Cleo, who had called me on the phone. "It have to come out."

"I not scared," I said.

"Oh," she said. Small pause, then, "That good," she said, finally.

And Jessie, who had come from Arima to go with me, stared at me with the biggest, widest eyes, asking, "Yuh okay, Jo? Yuh ready?"

I laughed. "I have to be, don't I?" I said.

She nodded abstractedly and motioned for James to take my bag up.

"Well, let's go then," she said, patting me on the small of my back.

And though I was glad for all this support, needed it in fact, when I stepped into the Nursing Home, it was like another Josephine took over.

Sure-footed, I left James and Jessie at reception without a backward glance and followed the nurses down the corridor. I felt nothing – no fear, no excitement – all I felt was the moment I was in and, with some intuition, I moved in harmony with it.

By the time James and Jessie came I was lying in bed, and while they fussed and worried, I found myself in some deep place I had not known existed before. Even the pain, which was coming more frequently and harder now, seemed such a part of me all I could do was feel it to the fullest. It is hard to describe now, but this pain that I rode, that I felt in every corner of my body, seemed also to be beyond me, outside somewhere, as we joined and parted at the same time. They said afterwards that I was in this intense labour for hours. They said the baby's head would not come down and everybody was worried. Mummy had called England and America and all my sisters were praying for me, saying a trans-Atlantic rosary. I vaguely remember my doctor coming in and talking his usual stupidness, but I was too tired for ol' talk; I did, however, notice the worried look on his face, and how he called James out the room after him. But these things were outside of my consciousness, I saw them as if from a distance, and with some vague sense that they were there, but their presence was like a turned-on television in an empty room.

Time itself had no impact on my consciousness, all I know is that eventually I got tired and asked the nurse for an injection to make me sleep. She in turn had looked at me worriedly.

"You sure?" she had asked, looking from me to James to Jessie.

I nodded, not needing to consult anyone as I so often did.

"But you taking the pain so good," she said.

"Is not the pain," I said. "I tired. I want to sleep."

"Okay," she said, "once yuh sure."

"I sure," I said, turning on my side so she could inject my hip. I closed my eyes when I saw the massive horse needle about to enter me. And, almost instantly, blissful sleep hit me. The medication and the pain were equally strong. Each contraction would wake me and then I would go into the deepest sleep after.

At some point a nurse came for me and I found myself being walked into the operating theatre. I remember Jessie's wide eyes looking at me as she asked the nurse if they were sure they had to cut me.

"What?" I said dazedly, looking from her to James. "What? No. No, James, I doh want a C-section."

As I put my foot into the room, another nurse appeared.

"Take her back," she said to the nurse holding me, "Doctor just call, he say to wait."

They turned and led me back to my room.

I don't know how much later it was when, somewhere in this drugged state, I touched my belly, and felt this immense connection to the baby inside me, the baby I suddenly knew was a son, and I whispered, "Come down, come down, my son."

And then I turned to Jessie and told her I needed to use the toilet.

"Nurse!" called Jessie excitedly. "I think she ready!"

The nurse bustled in looking shocked and happy at the same time.

"She ready?" she asked Jessie.

The women nodded, a look passed between them. I seemed to be sensing rather than seeing things, and I could sense their surprise.

And then everything seemed to be happening quickly. I was lying down, my doctor suddenly appeared. James stood at my side, rubbing my back, and as the first gush of blood splattered my doctor's gown, I closed my eyes. The pain was a red-hot fire I had to get out. I found myself pushing with strength I didn't know I had, like I woke up with this giant within me.

"Oh my God!" James said. "Look! Look! It coming, Doc!"

I opened my eyes and glanced down, but there was too much blood. I leant back and closed my eyes. Another big push.

"OH MY GOD!" James again. "OH GOD, JO! LOOK! IT TURNING! JESUS!!"

And there was another push, and suddenly my son was out. I could vaguely feel James planting a wet, slushy kiss on my cheek as he screamed, "I'm a father! Oh God, I'm a father!"

Somewhere in the background I heard a little cry, and my doctor saying, "Is a boy!" And I felt completely spent as if I had done a month's work in a moment.

And then the warmest, smallest, wettest little thing was placed on my belly, and I looked at my son for the first time and fell madly, stupidly and completely in love, and all the tiredness and pain now made sense.

When they took him back all I wanted was sleep. Peace and quiet and sleep. Jessie came in and hugged me, but I could barely respond. It was as if all my emotions had been used up. All that was left was the tears on my face that had fallen about the time I held my son.

James ran out of the room to call everyone he could think of, he couldn't care less that it was ten minutes to two in the morning. Only days later did I find out that my doctor had told James he would have to cut me if I didn't deliver by two o'clock.

Often, when I look back at certain moments in my life, I am struck by how powerful the moment was, how life-changing. That moment of birth was not only one of birth for my son, but one for me as well, the birth of a woman. In it and through it I found a self that was resilient and self-reliant, and, in its most vulnerable moment, most powerful. There seemed to be some comprehension of truly letting go and of being held up: The

162

Promise fulfilled. Yet, despite the power of self I felt that time in my life, it didn't take me long to fall back into the old patterns of self-doubt and dependence, only staying true in my mission to tackle motherhood consciously, to not let it just happen, as I'd done with so many other moments in my life, to take control; but I still had not addressed that trembling inside me.

Set Me Free

∞∞∞

It is August 1st, Emancipation Day in Trinidad and Tobago, and I am being freed of the last strings that tied my three-month-old foetus to me. Of course, being under anaesthesia, I feel nothing – nothing of the scraping, the emptying, of my inside. Nothing physical, that is.

I should have left.

Soon as Angie said she had German measles, I should have left. James had pulled me aside and said harshly, "Let us go!"

But I had vacillated.

"I won't see Bernie again before she goes back to England if I leave now," I'd pleaded.

"How she could come here with that?" he'd snapped back at me, angry with Angie for her selfishness.

"I know," I'd said, "but listen, we not sure that I really pregnant."

"That doh matter. Remember the time I had red-eye? I couldn't even cross yuh mother's gate. Now Angie come for lunch with German measles?"

I smiled foolishly. It was true; this favouritism among the sisters that my mother showed was extended in more ways than one. I remembered Bernie herself shouting, "Doh let him come here with that!"

Now she was sitting and laughing at the table with Angie. They all were. And the only concern, voiced by me, had been treated lightly as Bernie had asked if I was pregnant and my reply that I wasn't sure was met with, "Nah. Doh worry about it."

I had felt unease and annoyance, but had let it ride; discouraged so often from trusting and defending myself, I had ignored my feelings. Now James's justified anger was goading me into action. And even though we'd eventually left, we'd stayed too long. Long enough for me to contract German measles and, yes, I was pregnant.

When the phone rang early Wednesday morning, I picked it up with dread.

"Hello?" I said, my voice full of trepidation.

"Hello," said a perky voice on the other end, "I'd like to speak to Josephine Chin, please?"

"Speaking," I said, hopeful because this voice was too warm to be bringing bad news.

"Oh, hello. I'm calling from Saviour's Nursing Home. Your blood test results are ready. We've sent them up to your doctor."

To my doctor?

"Is everything all right?" I forced myself to ask.

"Your doctor will discuss it with yuh," said the stupid, perky voice. "Thanks. Goodbye!"

I stared at the phone, knowing something was wrong. I'd collected my blood test results myself when I was pregnant with my son. Why did my doctor have them now? With leaden legs I went to find James.

"You want to go now?" he asked.

I shrugged.

"Might as well," he said. "We might be worrying for nothing."

But we weren't. My tests showed I'd contracted German measles. I sat staring at my doctor as he explained every single, horrible effect of this on the foetus, and before he was halfway through I was sobbing loudly.

"I've seen these babies," I heard him say. "They suffer more if they're born."

I covered my face and shook my head.

165

"You can't be sure," I begged. "Yuh can't be sure mine will be like that."

"The chances of it being normal are almost nil. You have to do this. It will be too late in a couple of weeks."

"Yuh saying she should abort, Doc?"

I heard James's voice somewhere behind me.

"Yes," said my doctor firmly. "Yes. In cases like this, we always recommend it."

I could feel the room getting bigger as I shrank into myself. All I could do was bend my head and sob on the desk. I heard nothing he said after that. I was vaguely aware of James rubbing my back, helping me up, walking me out of the door. Only when he held out some medication to me did I come to life and slap his hand away.

As we got home, I could see James going more and more into himself, hiding in his anger and silence, now, when I needed him most. This made me angry and, together with the anger I felt towards Angie, I could feel my insides boiling and bubbling like a pressure cooker about to explode.

Later that night, after I had taken those innocent-looking little pills, we lay in front of the television.

Waiting.

By the time the labour pains started, he was snoring.

"James," I said, elbowing him.

No answer.

"James!" harder now.

"What," he said drowsily.

"It starting."

He turned and rubbed my belly, each circle slowing till it stopped. I realized he was still asleep. The pains were coming hard and fast. After a while it took too much effort to keep waking him. I could barely keep my wits about me, knowing this pain was for nothing, no reward at the end.

Miraculously, or maybe not, after an hour or so I felt a gush about to come. I got to the toilet just in time, as what looked like a massive period clot popped out of me. I sat there, waiting to hear it fall into the bowl. After a while I stood up. To my horror, the foetus clung to me by one tiny thread.

"James!" I called, but all I could hear was him snoring. I sat back on the bowl, and bounced my body up and down, trying to get it to let me go.

"James!" I called again, frantic now, terrified at how alone I was. There was no answer. From somewhere deeper than my heart a loud, guttural sound came, my pain, a massive unreachable blob inside me, was clinging to me, clinging enough for both of us, clinging with strength I, as mother, had not shown. What must have been an iota of time seemed like a lifetime to me, as loneliness and sorrow and hurt echoed inside me with so much force they drowned out every other sound, every other possibility, and made me hollow.

Eventually I took some toilet paper and put my hand between my legs and grabbed, my eyes so full of tears I could see nothing.

I pulled and then …

I let it go.

"Goodbye, my son," I said somewhere inside me, though I had not the courage to look at the still warm, bloody mass.

And then I bawled.

And then James came.

Now here I was, dead, as they scraped the last of my son out of me. Who and what he would have been only God knows. I have tormented myself many times with the what-ifs of life, for though I believe in a woman's choice, this was not my choice. I had no choice. I couldn't help asking myself who was I to judge if he was good enough to live? Why didn't I leave that day? What if he was normal and fine? And this anger at life's unfairness, this anger for Angie and her selfishness, for James who had slept through all of my pain, what was I to do with it?

I awoke from the anaesthetic feeling a ravenous hunger. The nurse looked at me with shock and disapproval when I asked for food. No, I didn't want painkillers, no, no antidepressants, no, not my husband, just food. And when they brought the food and I took two spoonfuls and became full, I realized that my hunger was not going to be so abated, that the hollow in my stomach would not be filled or fooled by food.

When I got home and James lost himself in front the television, I could feel my heart hardening. Ironically, the women around me ignored my pain. Only George, my brother-in-law, the one everyone always said was so insensitive, only he came to me with eyes full of compassion and sorrow, lost for words. He muttered my name and hugged me, and I loved him for that, that ability to share despite the helplessness he felt. Not even my husband had given me that. I felt lonely and betrayed. With five sisters, there was none I felt I could talk to. Once, another time, another loss, I had longed for people to shut up and leave me alone. Now, I longed for some words of comfort, some understanding, some hugging and holding. Though my friends called, though James efficiently brought me dinner in bed and took care of our son, there was no one I could bawl with, no one I could break down with. My husband hid behind the duties and tasks of the day, just as my mother had done when I was a child. Just as the child had longed for some comfort, the woman, now, yearned for the same thing, and I sadly acknowledged that I had married my mother.

All I wanted to do was bawl and be held until I could stop.

And there was no one I could do it with.

Same old society that had shown its callous face to a broken sixteen-year-old, reared again. Put on a smiling face, just pretend,

pretend, pretend. Even those closest around me wanted that; no one wanted to hear my anger, to hear me cast blame or voice the doubt I felt. My mother never bothered to ask how I was; instead she talked about how wrong abortion was and how I should have had more faith. Consumed by his own anger, his own sense of injustice, James treated me as though I was invisible. I could feel myself growing hard and cold and hating him.

Days became a long tedious time of abnormal normalcy, and nights a continuous replay of the same horror movie: a little, curled up body, hanging on to me by that one string. My two-year-old son found I had no time for him, no patience. Mummy played no more tickle games, she bathed him and read for him and walked him, but she hugged him from far away and she didn't really smile and she seemed to be looking at something else, someone else. He would reach up and touch my face, his little hand soft and warm, his eyes wide, searching mine.

"I love you, Mummy," he would say, the magic words that always made Mummy giddy with glee.

And Mummy would say, "I love you too, son."

But he could not feel her glee. Only her sadness.

It was a few weeks later when James came to me holding out a ticket.

"Wha's this?" I said.

"A ticket. To New York."

I stared at him.

"What for? Where yuh get this?"

"Is for you," he said, flapping it at me. "You need to get away for a while."

"Where I going?" I asked.

"By Mary," he said. "Is all arranged."

"We doh have money for this," I said, steupsing.

"Doh worry about that. It bought aready."

"Yuh know we can't afford this, James," I said angrily, turning away.

We were in the process of building our house; every dollar was accounted for.

James grabbed my hand and spun me around.

"No," he said, "no. We can't afford this. But we can afford you falling apart on us even less. Yuh son need yuh. I need yuh."

I stared at him. All the desertion I'd felt that night washed over me and flooded my eyes.

"How dare you?" I hissed. "How dare you make plans for my life like this? Now yuh coming? Now? Where the hell yuh was when I needed yuh? Send me away – so yuh doh have to deal with me, right?"

I was shaking, it took all my effort not to reach up and slap him.

"Josephine," he said, suddenly crumbling before me. He spread his arms out.

"I sorry. I – I just couldn't deal with it. I was vex' with her, with you for staying, with God, with *everybody!* With this whole shitting mess. I didn't know what to do, how to fix it …"

"You should have been there!" I snapped.

He bowed his head.

"I know," he said, "I know. But look, I trying to fix it now."

He held the ticket out to me.

I turned away, my anger washed away, at least for now, by his eyes – his eyes that reminded me of another man who had turned suddenly old and tired before my eyes. Another man who couldn't get the time to fix it, whose daughter never got the time to know him. A warning bell went off inside me. Some fear that I didn't want to be the one responsible for another man's breaking, another man not getting a chance.

"Okay," I said, turning around. "Okay, I'll go."

No one knew the don't-give-a-damn attitude I went with. The sudden terrifying feelings that came upon me often, the ones that made me feel like I was dying, that had stopped me from going out many times, and kept me in a constant prison, these I threw out of the window now. I couldn't care less if I did die; I had nothing to live for. With bitterness and nonchalance, I packed my bags and left with my sister-in-law, Liz, for Mary and her husband in New York.

The general plan was to keep me busy, shopping, sightseeing, talking, liming, whatever it took to bring me back to myself. And it was hard not to be full of life around Mary – always teasing, full-of-mischief Mary. When I got to her house the first night and she'd organized for her brothers-in-law – who I used to lime with when I was younger – to be there, along with Lyn, my brother's ex-wife, and a big pot of good-tasting Trini pelau was bubbling on the stove, I could feel my instinct to laugh and talk, that survivor instinct within me, peeping out.

A couple of days later I was mall shopping and fast-food eating and the pace of life in America got me going. Yet I didn't really bounce back. I was hungry for true conversation about what had happened and how I felt, but no one seemed to want to hear. Everyone assumed that the best therapy was for me to move on and forget, and the women around me, being older and perhaps wiser, probably knew no amount of talking would lessen the pain. But for me, getting lost in something else was not the answer. I did not know it then, and I just fell into the pattern of pretence that they, with the best intentions, ordained; but now I know I needed to honour that loss by letting it wrap me up for a while and to acknowledge, not ignore it.

I longed for the wisdom of the East that allows for official mourning, a time when people are expected to gnash their teeth, to weep, to hold mournful prayer and song sessions, for the world to see, not in quiet, not in hiding. Our wakes that we have in Trinidad when someone dies usually end up being an all-fours and rum lime. No – this festers my anger about the shallow and unfeeling world we live in. If I need to cry, then cry with me, do not tell me how to do it and when to stop.

So I participated in New York life and played the role, but inside I knew that when no one was looking I would crawl into a corner and be sad. And in the middle of a mall one day, it hit me. Standing in the changing room, I suddenly felt my legs weaken, my heart start to race, my breath shorten, as I had one fleeting thought: everybody dies.

I quivered about my lost baby, my dead father, the husband I had left behind, my son at home, Simone, Lynton, everybody had left me. And then the room started spinning, closing in on me. I had had many smaller incidents like this, lasting little time and from which I had recovered quickly, but this one was bad, like the night I'd been going out with Jessie. I stumbled out of the dressing room, weak, barely able to look around for Mary and Liz, saying over and over in my mind, *God, please, don't let me die*. The concern on their faces was like Jessie's that night, it made me feel foolish and frightened.

"You want to go to the hospital?" asked Mary.

I shook my head no.

"I just want to leave," I said.

Everybody was panicked.

"Okay," said Mary. "Okay, let's get you home."

I could feel their energy changing, changing because of me. They were worried, frightened, upset.

"Let me hold yuh bags," said Liz. "Yuh sure yuh doh want to stop and get something to eat or drink?"

"No. No." I shook my head. I just wanted to get back to Mary's place, safe and sound.

So upset they were that Mary lost her bearings and we nearly caused an accident on the freeway. Eventually, we met back up with the long, tree-lined road that led to her house and I could feel myself calming down.

"You want something to eat or drink, Jo?" Mary asked when we got home.

"No, no. I just want to lie down."

Now that I was here I no longer felt those weird feelings, just an incredible tiredness.

Mary looked intensely at me.

"Yuh feeling better, Jo?"

I nodded.

"Soon as yuh reach home yuh feeling better, ent?"

"Well …" I said uneasily, "I started to when we left the mall …"

She nodded.

"Anxiety," she said.

"What?" I asked, staring at her.

"Yuh getting anxiety attacks, panic attacks."

"Why? How yuh know is that?"

"Because I used to get them," she said, "and I know the symptoms. Yuh suddenly get scared, have to get out or get up, go back home?"

I nodded, feeling embarrassed.

"How yuh stop it?" I finally asked.

"Pray. I prayed it away."

"God!" I said. "I feel foolish!"

"No," said Liz, coming up and rubbing my back.

"Lots of people have it in America," Mary reassured me. "In fact it was my boss who told me what was happening with me, he used to have them too. There are centres for research up here for it."

"So … I mad then?" I asked.

"Not at all!" said Liz behind me.

"No, no, Jo, is not madness," said Mary, "is fear."

"Of what?" I whispered, knowing that I was afraid of many things.

"Mainly death, dying," said Mary.

I nodded.

"Yes, that sound like it," I said eventually.

"Doh worry," said Mary, "I'll order some information on it that will stop it, and send it for yuh in Trinidad."

I bowed my head, feeling tears coming.

My sister hugged me as Liz patted my back.

"Doh worry, Jo, I think is something we all have, in the family, yuh know. A late reaction to Daddy's death and all that. Just overwhelming fear – fear of things we see and hear. Anyway, now yuh know why yuh had to come here."

Now I know why my baby had to die too, I thought to myself, without that I would never have been here. Fear would have kept me at home. Safe. So my baby had to die to bring me back to life then, not life on the surface like I'd been living it, not life full of fear, but life in its fullness. How harsh and ironic life can be.

Right Turn

~~~~~

Sitting in the audience, way in the back, waiting for my turn to go on stage now, I silently thank Mary. Had it not been for her and the package that arrived for me a few weeks after my return to Trinidad, I would not be sitting here. I would have fled long ago, thinking the palpitations and sweaty palms and dizziness were a sure sign I was dying.

Now, as the age-old anxiety that had threatened me for so long pumped through every part of my being, I sat still, chanting the mantras that the material told me would take me out of this state. Between that and the prayers I said, I managed to sit out the first half and, barely keeping my wits about me, I ventured outside at intermission. In between my attempts at self-hypnosis, I kept telling myself I should just go home. Why was I putting myself through this terror? I even went up to James, who was there with my nephews, telling him I wasn't sure I wanted to do this again.

But he shook his head and ignored my escape arguments.

"If yuh doh want to do it again after today that's fine, but do it today, we here already."

With my legs weak and my breath ragged, I went backstage into the dressing room. I kept swigging my honey and lime mixture, feeling my throat closing up on me, sniffing shiling oil, anything to keep myself distracted. When the person who was on just before me went on stage, I could distract myself no more: this was it.

The moment.

God, I prayed, staring at my frightened eyes in the mirror, barely able to look at myself long enough to touch up my lipstick. *God, please, hold me up. Don't let me fall or die or anything,* I begged. *Hold me up like you did when I went to have my son, fill me with that confidence you gave me then. Please, God, please, I beg you.*

I could hear the applause. I could hear the MC introducing me. I wiped my sweating palms on the sides of my dress and walked onto the stage.

I stood in the centre of the stage, in front the mike; the floodlights blinded me.

I spread my arms, took a breath, and began.

> "Conscious –
> mean yuh conscience must make yuh see,
> through the veil, a society …"

I began to feel myself grow with each word, feel my poetry fill me, make me breathe, till I had the feeling of being above, looking down, and now I could see the audience.

> "Not all tings, is reality.
> Doh follow de custom an' jus' succumb,
> Look at destruction, youths causing ruction …"

I had the feeling of the most complete freedom I have ever felt, a feeling like I was dancing at last, hearing at last, some rhythm inside me that had been playing softly, and now it was loud, loud. And it was the tune my body had been waiting to hear all along.

> "They shooting fer fun,
> But we is de one,
> Who buy dem de gun.
> When he is a boy, we say, is a toy,
> When he turn man, yuh could take it from he han'?"

As I ended I had the distinct feeling of my feet hitting the floor, and it took me a while to realize the audience was standing and screaming and that I had walked off and was being pushed back onto the stage. In a daze I performed again, walked off, changed my clothes, collected my stuff in the dressing room, walked round the building and slipped back into the audience.

"That was real good, sister," said Brother Resistance as I passed him.

"Thanks," I said, too enraptured to say more, whispering then a thank you to the miracle that had given me that moment.

They told me afterwards that no one had ever got that kind of response in the history of Breaking New Ground, a show featuring new, up-and-coming rapso artistes. I knew my piece was good, but I also knew that I'd had great spirit help that night, that somewhere hidden inside me this talent, that I had tapped into quite by chance, had been like a light inside me, suddenly uncovered, showing me the truth of who I could be.

Showing me the spirit I had forgotten.

As destiny would have it, 'Conscious' pulled me all over the place. I found myself having to walk the talk so each time I performed, I faced my demons, shivering with fear as I waited to go on stage and exulting in that all-powerful force that not only held me up but made me magnificent, that force that had saved me so many times before, and I understood that I would do it again and again, despite my fear, because it was who I was meant to be. I found myself in schools throughout Trinidad and Tobago, at companies' Emancipation Day celebrations, and, eventually, 'Conscious' took me on television. Early the following year, I performed it at the sixth International Conference of Caribbean Women Writers and Scholars and for the Governor General of Grenada.

Before I left for Grenada I was filled with the greatest anxiety; the mere idea that I was leaving the island made anxiety attacks come on in a big way. Even though my safe zone, James, was going with me, I couldn't stop thinking that the plane would crash or that, if not death itself, I'd have something else really bad happen to me. I tried to rein in the thought, digging into me, that this was too good to be happening to me; memories of another time consumed me, the memories of looking around for that terrible thing coming towards me, of stopping my joy so that sorrow would not come. I could barely keep my wits about me in the airport, on the plane, on landing in Grenada. For a moment I was swept away by the beauty of the Renaissance Hotel; remembering my days as a seasoned traveller with Mummy, I roamed the grounds and walked on the white sand, but the nagging thought that I had to perform the next night kept me from enjoying it all.

On the night of the performances at the Governor General's house, I was so panicked I could hold no conversations; as people milled about and some came up to talk, I found myself walking off, tempted to take a stiff drink but then changing my mind lest I made a complete fool of myself. I nodded distractedly at James, who tried to pull me into a conversation about the beauty of the old colonial home we were in, and eventually found myself in an obscure little corner, waiting.

When it was my turn to go on, I felt to bolt, my legs could barely hold me up. I looked desperately at James, willing him to take my arm and just lead me out of there to somewhere safe. Instead, he watched me and gave me a smile, a thumbs up, and then he leant back, waiting. I prayed so hard God must have personally come down for me that night. I begged harder than I'd ever done, for strength. And, as I stood at the podium and opened my mouth, a breeze hit me from behind, slammed into my back with such force that I grabbed the edges of the table. The breeze pushed back the microphone and whistled into it, sizzled through the room as I lifted my voice and began my piece.

I felt if I just let go enough, gave into this breeze enough, I would fly. And the applause that rocked the room after I was done, like thunder after the storm of fear that I had just weathered, made me think, for one second, that perhaps I did. Fly.

Yet, before the trip was done, I was giving less and less attention to this phenomenal experience as faith and fear jostled for position inside my mind and old habits, engrained in me since birth, rose to precedence. By day five, I couldn't wait to get back home, to the safety of Trinidadian shores.

As 'Conscious' took me on this spinning whirlwind of creativity, I found myself in meetings with Trinidadian greats like Ras Shorty I and Andre Tanker. I found myself in studios and on stage performing with these icons, being asked to give talks and put on shows and talking recording possibilities. And as the pace became more and more hectic, I became more and more alarmed by everything, awed by it all.

"*Wait!*" I said silently. "Wait a minute! This is all happening too fast!"

In my mind's eye, I put up my hand, stopping it all, shielding myself from it all. And, as I'd requested, the Universe listened, and it all came to a grinding halt before I realized it. Everything stopped. For years.

Broken Wings

∞∞∞

I am sitting in the park near to my home, leaning against a giant, comforting tree and torturing myself with the end of year ritual I have of contemplating my life. It is at times like these when the volume rises inside me and I am aware of the echo of those words, given to me so long ago that night in my father's car when my world seemed about to blow up, those quiet words of wisdom, *Happiness is inside you.*

And then I see it – this red and brown butterfly darting in front me, flitting around me before settling on the tree next to mine.

"Hi," I whisper as, I swear, it watches me.

I see that one of its wings is torn, not quite whole, and then it lifts off and is gone.

I don't believe in making New Year's resolutions any more, so it is with some surprise that, as I get up and dust my bottom, I find myself vowing to pursue my happiness during the coming year.

And then, on Christmas morning, the tiniest package rips me open. Sterling silver earrings from Liz, butterfly earrings, attached to a card that reads:

Happiness … Joyful spirit … fly free …

I find myself grinning as I put on my butterfly earrings.

Some weeks later Mummy and I go to Mount St Benedict to spend the day. We walk into the church and sit down, me one pew in front her. I turn to ask her for her Daily Word and, as she passes it to me, something falls to the ground. I bend and pick up the bookmark which reads "Oh Lord of all life, give my heart wings …" and I flip it over to see a picture of a butterfly hatching out of its cocoon. I gasp.

"Can I keep this?"

Mummy nods.

Before we leave I drag her into the abbey shop.

"Let's get something," I say, "some token of our day."

"Okay," she says, smiling.

We enter the shop and, as I turn towards the counter to see what I want, there facing me is a wall of butterfly pins in every imaginable colour.

"What does it mean?" I say.

Mummy squeezes my hand.

"I suppose it has something to do with change. You should get one."

I turn to the cashier.

"I'll take two pins," I say, "one for me and one for my mom."

Later that year, in direct pursuit of this elusive happiness, I enter my first short story competition. I have entered many poetry competitions and have been well received in this genre, but my prose, for all I know, might be considered utter crap. Ten winners will be chosen from this competition to attend a three-week creative writers' workshop. Unable to write anything new, I pull out the story I'd written on my dad years before, polish it up and send it off. And then I wait … fervently, adamantly, wearing my butterfly earrings.

And eventually it comes … a white envelope in the mail …

While we recognize the strength of your work … unable to give you a place … try again … good luck …

My brain picked out words like bullet holes in the paper.

"Doh study them," said James when he eventually found me in the bathroom and pulled me to him. "I mean, what they know? Is the whole art thing, yuh know?"

I nodded at his chest, just to get him to leave me alone. Instead he pulled me off him and looked me in the eye.

"You're a damn good writer. Yuh hear?"

I nodded again at the space behind his shoulder. He shook me.

"Josephine. You're a damn good writer. Doh let nothing take away that."

"Okay," I said, exasperated. "I just wish someone else besides you would find so."

"It will come. Just forget them and write yuh book, okay?"

I scoffed. Write my book? After this?

"Okay," I said. "Sure."

"I'll give yuh a couple of weeks to get over this. Then I expect to see yuh writing."

"Really?" I said, stepping back and glaring at him. "Or else what?"

"Or else," he said, pulling me back to him, "or else you'll have to go back and teach."

"What kind of shitty ultimatum is that?" I said, pushing him away. "Who yuh think you are to run my life so?"

"Just yuh husband," he said, smiling, "and right now, yuh logic. And is not a ultimatum, just a reality check. Yuh leave teaching to write, so if yuh not writing, go back and teach."

I steupsed and walked off, his cool practicality angering me more, reminding me of another man who brought reason to my world when I needed chaos as my cover.

Of course we both knew that now, just for spite, I would let more than two weeks pass without writing, and I would make sure he knew. But we also both knew September was little over a month away, and that was the beginning of the new school term.

And then, before I had time to demonstrate my rebellion, the fateful phone call came that set me walking on another path of my life. The phone call that told me that one of the ten winners couldn't make it and I was next on the list; the phone call that asked if I was still interested in attending the workshop.

"Yuh see?" asked James. "Yuh see? Yuh believe me now?"

I laughed. "I thought they didn't know anything?"

"Well, they do now!"

But the euphoria didn't last long, because now I realized I'd be gone for three weeks, hours away from James, with no phone, no car – cut off and far away – and unable to be reached when anxiety got me.

I didn't dare say anything to James, who had once told me I was both ways wrong – miserable if I didn't get something, afraid of it if I did. I had got really angry at the time; now that this was proving true, he was the last person I wanted to know, so I smiled and did what I was so good at – pretended.

"So," said James, coming up to me on the night before I was to leave, pressing his hands into my shoulders as I stuffed things in and pulled them out of my bag. "So, Jo. Yuh know this is a once in a lifetime opportunity?"

I nodded, my packing (unpacking?) taking all my attention.

"Good," said James, lifting my face to him. "Good."

Well – that was that.

When I could pretend no more, I got up and stared at myself in the mirror. It was three in the morning. James's snores filled the room. In front of me, staring back at me, were these frightened child's eyes. I wished I had the rejection letter now to remind me of how I felt then and how I should be feeling now.

If you don't embrace these things they will stop, remember?

What's the worst thing that can happen?

I can die! the child screamed.

I stared at her, this child whose spirit had been called to order so much she had become afraid of it.

I became filled with sadness for her.

No, I said. *No. I won't let you die.*

Doubtful eyes stared back at me, slowly she smiled back at me a little, and trusted me a little.

Me.

The adult now.

And that was how I eventually came to deal with anxiety. All before I had tried to conquer it, to stop it, even to fool it. Now I saw it, expected it, as part of the understanding of who I was and what I had learnt from life. I choose not to let anxiety stop me or control me, because, more than anything, I'm afraid that if I do let it, I will stop the gifts the Universe wants to give me, maybe this time for good. And I know now that this same anxiety allows me to be who I am today – compassionate, aware, resilient; without it I would have been a different person, more sure-footed, but far less believing in spirit.

Now as I write this final chapter, I am aware that, if I choose, this point can be one of closure and beginning. My novel has taken me on a journey of the past where I have come to recognize that this Chin identity, that I have felt all my life to be a burden, I understand and accept now. Whether this identity is a blessing or a curse is not the issue; now, more than anything, I am glad for the Chin name because of the stock it allows me to come from – resilient, unstoppable people who are never ashamed of their fear, who fight and work through their fear and who, through their fear, keep their humanity and hone their strength.

And starting this new road with me are this novel and a new baby who, I realize, will make me face everything I am afraid of. Just as my first son showed me the power of surrender, and my second son brought me emancipation, now this one brings me the understanding of choice – whether fear or faith will rule my life, as each morning I awake to go to the table next to my bed that is covered with cotton wool and needles and the dreaded scent of methylated spirits that has assailed my nostrils and filled me with fear and distrust ever since that orange-hued little girl was coloured in grey. Now this task of injecting myself with insulin is part of my routine. Some days my thighs seem so forested with dots that I can find nowhere to put the needle, other days my hand shakes so much I end up having to start over and over, leaving a trail of grazes along my leg. It never gets easier, and in a way this is good, because I never want what's not supposed to be easy to seem like it is because time says so. What I want is simply the wisdom of acceptance, and the knowledge that the only thing we really can have, in the face of everything, is hope.

James bends to kiss me, and I see in his eyes the fear that is usually in mine. And somehow I am the one squeezing his hand, telling him it'll be okay. As they wheel me in for my C-section I realize that I have no control over that big looming thing that has controlled so much of my life – all I can do is go with the process of life.

And then I am walking towards this bright light. Coming from it, straight into me, are my father's words, louder and louder until they vibrate from every part of my being. And then I hear another voice, and still another, calling me, and I open my eyes to a fluorescent light and James with one arm around Zack's shoulders and another around a tiny, red bundle.

"Hi, babe," he says, smiling.

"Hi, Mom," says Zack, bending and peering at my stomach.

"Hi," I say, feeling like I am walking on air. "Hi, guys."

James bends and puts the bundle on my shoulder, and I wince with the effort it takes to turn my head. And then I am looking into these eyes that stare back at me with so much knowledge that for a moment I am jolted out of my grogginess. I kiss son number three and every pain and problem pregnancy brought me is replaced by wonder and love and something else ... I close my eyes as the warmth of the light enfolds me, and now I am walking in it, walking with my children, my husband, my father's words, and then I recognize the feeling and finally, I understand that a butterfly with broken wings will still fly; I *understand* ... that happiness is a choice.

Glossary

anchar	achar; an Indian preserved condiment
bad hair	ethnic African hair, thick and difficult to comb
bobolee	innocent victim of ridicule, named after a stuffed effigy of Judas, formerly beaten on Good Friday
break	bankrupt
Brother Resistance	one of the Fathers of rapso
buss, bust	burst
buss style	to show off
candlefly	firefly
check	to date a girl regularly
chow	as in mango chow, half-ripe mango cut up and seasoned with salt, pepper and green seasoning
cut-eye	an eye and head movement expressing contempt
dada head	bad hair, knotty hair, ethnic African hair
doh	don't
dotish	stupid, unable to reason
doubles	popular snack of two bara (patties) sandwiching curried channa (chickpeas)
dreadlocks	the uncut, plaited or matted hair of the Rastafarian
duncy	stupid, a dunce

fete	party, dance, jump-up, usually with music and alcohol
fig	banana
gun-mouth	tapered
hard-headed	stupid, unteachable, obstinate
hickey	lovebite
horner-man	lover; man who cuckolds husbands
jep	large aggressive wasp with a severe and ready sting
jump-up	dance, usually with Carnival music and alcohol
ketch	catch
knotty hair	thick hair that tangles easily
lil	little
lime	casual social gathering
maco	watch inquisitively, spy
mamee	mummy, mother
mooksie	dotish, foolish, gullible
obeah	a system of belief in supernatural powers for or against evil
ol' talk, old talk	idle chatter, gossip
outside man	lover of a married woman
pastelle	cornmeal stuffed with pork, beef, raisins etc.
pelau	one-pot meal of rice, meat and vegetables
pores	*see* raised pores
pumpkin-vine family	extended family, not necessarily blood-related
pweffen	jocular slang for tail, waist, other part of the body
quite	all the way away, as far away as
raised pores	gooseflesh

rapso	Trinidad's rhythm poetry, described as the power of the word in the rhythm of the word, may or may not be accompanied by music
Rasta	member of the dreadlocked Rastafarian cult
Rastafarian	pertaining to the cult of Haile Selassi's divinity and the wickedness of Western-style society, or Babylon
red-eye	conjunctivitis
red man	a light brown-skinned person, of mixed black and white ancestry
run	to chase or drive away
shiling oil	a Chinese cure-all used for breathing problems
soca	a Trinidad invention, dance music with lyrics, a fusion of American SOul with Trinidad CAlypso
steups	sucking the teeth
stick the cake	to make the ceremonial first cut in a cake, to eat the first slice of cake together, often into a kiss
sweat rice	cooked rice laced with the sweat of a woman's undergarment
tie-tongue	lisp, speech impediment
up	in the north
UWI	University of the West Indies
wine	an erotic dance movement of hips and buttocks